we write
because we
need to
write!
we climb
mountains
to the
tippy top
to get to the
best view
and swim too
far out to
catch the
biggest wave.

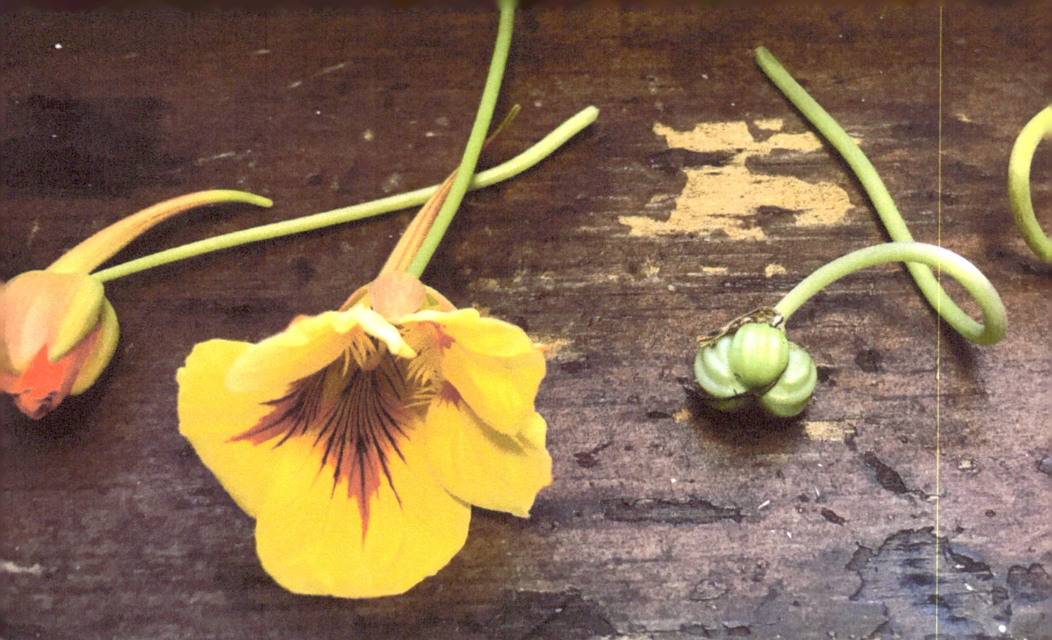

2

You Can't Spit Far in the Shower
© 2022 Copyright Karen Izzi.
All Rights Reserved.

ISBN 978-0-578-69018-6

Library of Congress Control Number: 2022918791

POEMS AND IMAGES
Karen Izzi © 2022. All rights reserved.
www.karenizziphd.org

PUBLICATION DESIGN
Brady Book Design
www.BradyBookDesign.com

COVER IMAGE
David Brady
www.BradyArt.com

Poem by Rainer Maria Rilke page 95

Printed in the United States

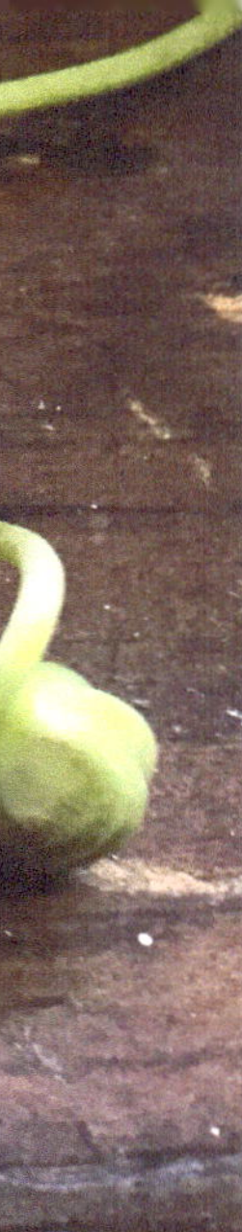

gratitudes

I offer sincere thanks to my parents, Tony and Patti Izzi, who are the most admirable couple, teachers, friends, and lifelong companions. For this bond, I am eternally grateful.

Phyllis Terry, my partner, who just laughs as I create, sing loudly, and dance around the house.

For my Grandmother, Rose Appicciafuoco Pompeo who was the keeper of my heart. From spending so much time together in the kitchen, we became best of friends. She knew me best.

Aunt Joann, my god-mother and best friend, love you to the moon, and every thrift store in between.

Lis Kalogris, you always encourage me, cheer me on, even from afar, to be my best creative self and never doubt a bit of it.

Christine Morby, my lifelong friend and creative proofreader, who shares such enormous faith.

Melody Templeton, Soul flame, you empower me well beyond my own good.

Jane Groves Hardy, you have taught me that something from nothing is more than anything else. Dance in the kitchen. Love hard or go home.

To you, who participate in my life and provide the inspiration to write it all down.

in praise of the poets

We write because we need to write! We climb mountains to the tippy top to get the best view and swim too far out to catch the biggest wave. As writers, we are curious and want answers, resolve. We touch without touching at all. We pause like statues in the middle of our busy, everyday lives to gather it all in. We write without fear, without knowing where we will end up. Sometimes, we create in the middle of the darkest night, scribble on water bottle labels, on our skin, and on discarded gum wrappers. We record every little thing that our heart takes in.

Writers continually bare their souls and hope that someone will pick us up...

Poets savor intuition and all the little bits of real life that we stumble upon. We bring wholeness to those who are broken, spark memories in those who have forgotten, and a smile to anyone who might be in need. Writers open their hearts to the whole wide world. Poetry offers the most magical expression, connects everyone everywhere at the same time. As we stumble, the written word becomes a steppingstone. In between the lines we find value in the truth, colorful bits, and scrappy pieces in black and white, like a hammock for the soul.

Oh, how different life is now, my journal, compared to the diary of a 12-year-old girl in 1918. This is our work. My first diary was a small, almost square floral book with gold-lined pages. It had a lock and key, which I kept around my neck on a silver chain through the 8th grade. I loved a boy named Andy, had my hands in flour with my grandmother, consoled my Poppop who had to bury his dog. I could not say "I love you" to my dad yet, wrote of sexual abuse and not having a voice. There were three proms in one season, bullying the neighborhood kid, and never feeling comfortable in a bathing suit. But, always, I dreamed of being a writer and artist.

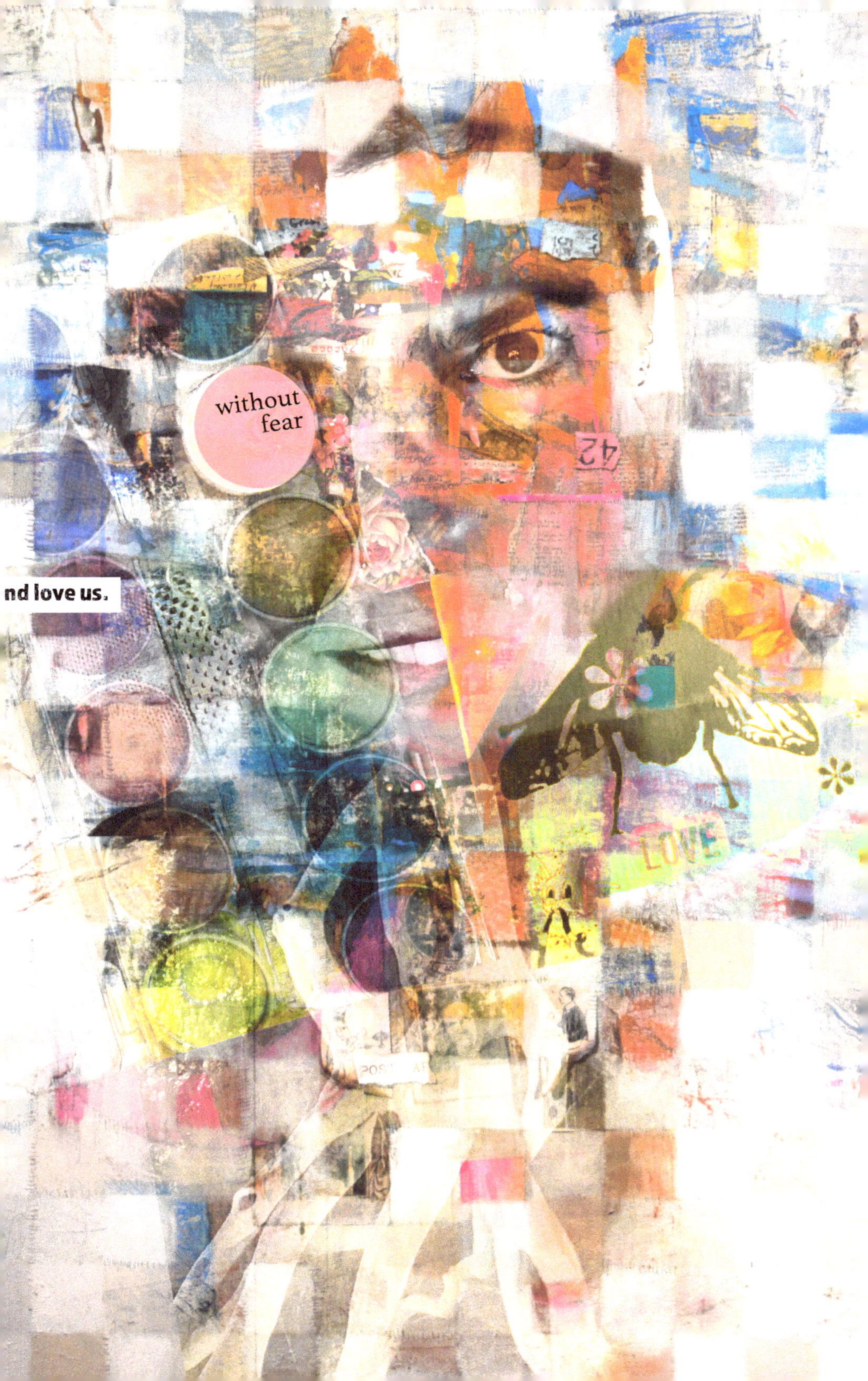

without fear
nd love us.
LOVE
42

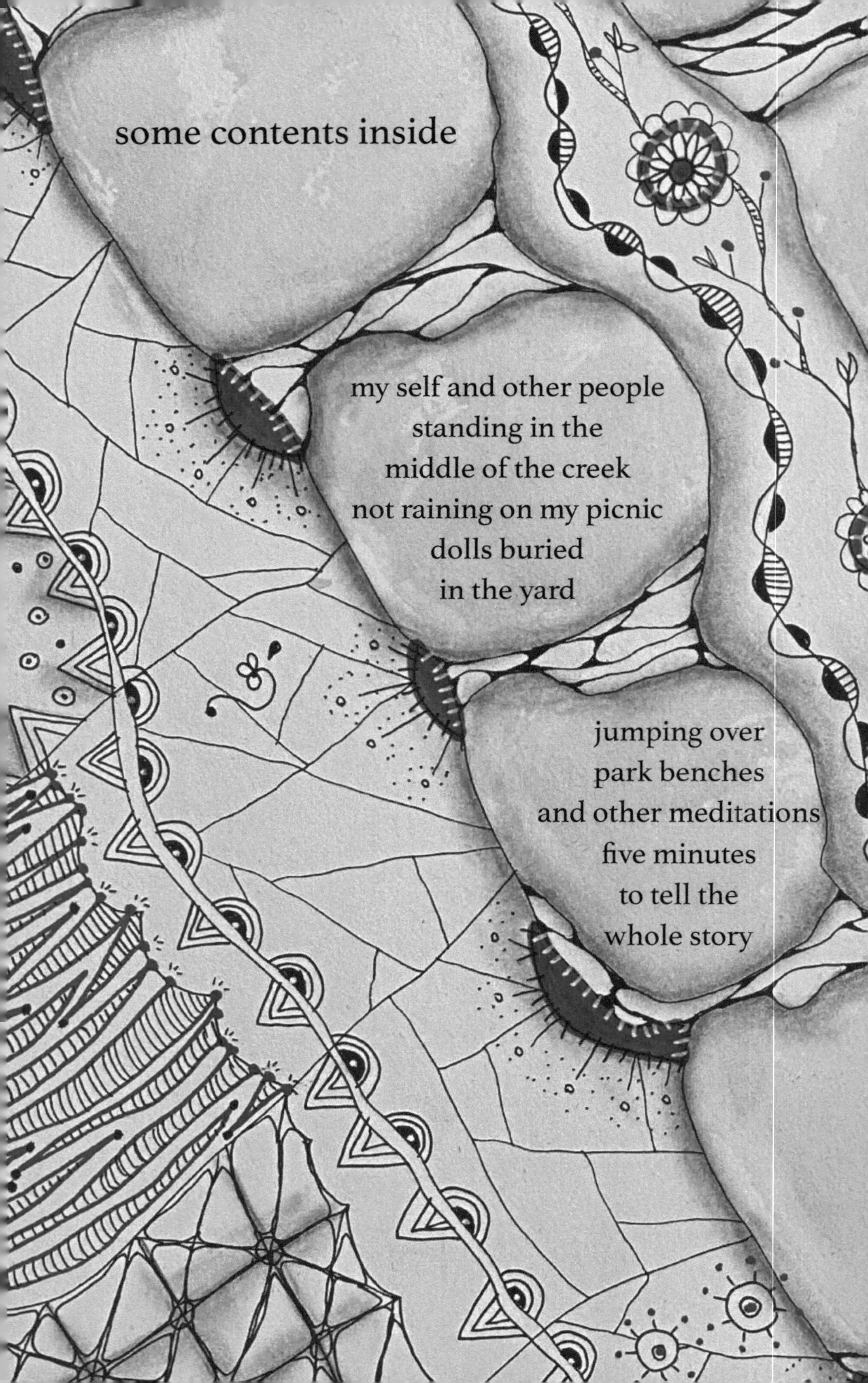

some contents inside

my self and other people
standing in the
middle of the creek
not raining on my picnic
dolls buried
in the yard

jumping over
park benches
and other meditations
five minutes
to tell the
whole story

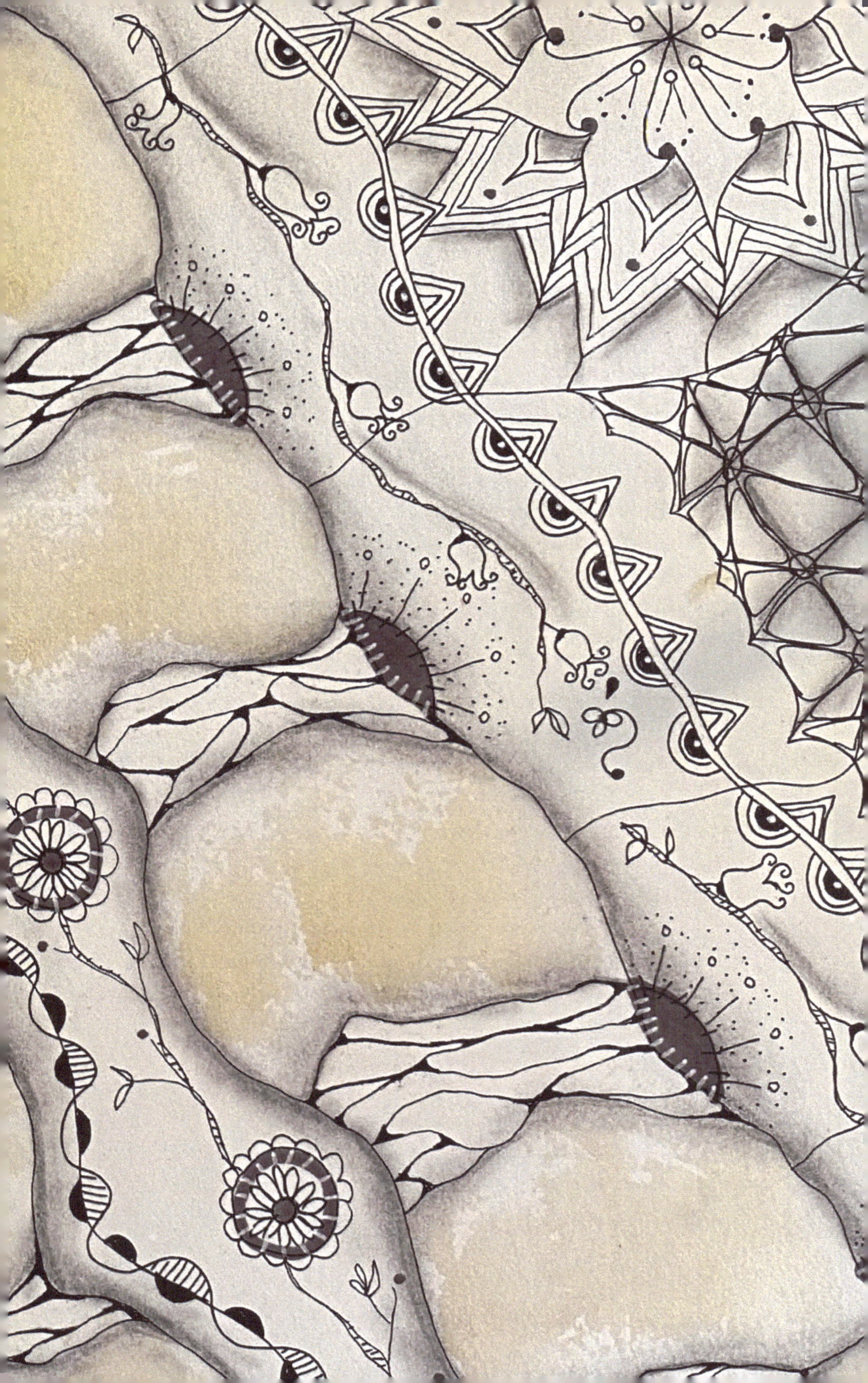

soul attraction

No, it's not just dry, hot, and barren. It is so much more than that. My list is long. I adore the desert, not only because I breathe better here, but because when I am here, I return to the time that stands still. I am my authentic self. I love the never-ending openness. My heart is so peaceful, clean, and uninhibited, just as these native lands.

When I climb tallest peaks, I am closer to spirit. It is my personal heaven. This morning I pass clusters of tiny white flowers, purple ones, steep banks loaded with boulders, and the classic bright yellow blooms of the palo verde trees. Against the big blue sky, they lead the way as I become closer to Mother Nature and her big horizon. I am a desert dweller from birth. I was drawing cactus and mountains before, Mom said, I ever knew what they were. I am one who loves plants, creatures big and small. It excites me every single time a lizard scoots across my path. I love the voyage through the swirling dust and dirt as it moves around me. A force that moves me. I thrive under the cobalt blue sky.

At any time of the year, the desert is blooming with color, full color. The physical beauty and uniqueness of the mountains in front of me shows off its variety of hues. Like pieces of a quilt they are sewn together to become part of a larger picture. They change color throughout the day as the sun shifts and shadows dance along. What I always find breathtaking are the plants and trees that grow from tiny cracks and crevices. The light shines on the boulders and from the smallest crack brilliant plants sprout, survive and thrive. Really makes me think.

It requires an open mind to rise to notice and appreciate the miracle of this place. The existence and miraculous survival of all its wildlife and plant life. I am quite sure that I have a spiritual connection to this land. Perhaps I have lived here in a past life.

Geographically, the land has transformed and reinvented itself over the past few million years. Surfaces, layers, altitudes, different visual landscapes, and perspectives have perplexed scientists for the history of the land. We continue to notice and record changes in the sun's exposure, areas of extreme development and lack of percipitation. Certainly, global warming is a threatening area of conversation.

I sit here, alone, considering my physical location. I suddenly feel special, so fortunate to be right here, right now. I am currently part of the grand and magical space. I choose a boulder beneath a mesquite tree. Wispy leaves catch the breeze and offer my body relief from the heat. There is no need to use my voice here. The greetings that I receive from nature are all I need.

Part of the admiration of this colorful, arid place is my love and fascination with Saguaro cactus. The first time that I stood up tall next to an old Saguaro for a picture, I was 19 years old. It made me realize my smallness, my ego, and my slumped shoulders. I sensed the energy that drew me near. Then I felt the sudden prick on my sweaty back as I backed up a bit too close. Carnegiea gigantea, Saguaro, is only found in the Sonoran Desert regions of the United States and Mexico. No other place in the world. It is illegal to harm, harvest, cut, or collect them. A ten-year-old Saguaro is only about 1.5" tall, sprouting beneath a tree or shrub for protection. Easy to miss if you aren't mindful on your trek. Adult Saguaros have pleats, or ribs, that allow them to expand as they take in moisture. Year after year, those late spring, white, waxy blossoms continue to amaze me.

I fetch a journal and pen from my pack and make an additional attempt to record the colors, sounds, and emotions that I have found here, hundreds of times. I make friends with birds, reptiles, and even a passing cloud. I am transformed among the ancient grounds. I study, with great respect, the petroglyphs nearby. I get it. The innate need to communicate what we see, hear, and learn here. Each time I visit this spot, not too much has changed since the time before, including my desire to pick up a pen to write and record. I write about the rocks and arrangement of their perfect alignment. Even their breaks are perfect, giving life to unbelievably successful flowers. I consider their strong root systems that have learned to collect and store just the right amount of water to survive the hottest summer months. Then I wonder if I am the only one who notices.

I unwind and enjoy an apple to rehydrate. Deliberately, I sit perched half in the sun and half in the shade. My lungs are able to completely expand and clean out. Next to me I notice that someone has arranged steppingstones leading down, six or eight feet, to a sandy wash. Washes are the carved out, dried out, riverbeds that have been created during the monsoon season. Water rushes these washes carrying treasures like rocks, sticks, and once in a while a special treasure. Now, blades of grass have held onto droplets of water. I always like to take the road less traveled. I seek out heart shaped rocks for my personal collection and often find fossils and small shells. I know, right? How many people miss out by staying on the trails? I have met large desert tortoises, Gila monsters, rattlers, scorpions, hawks, and many I have not identified.

No, I don't mind being alone in the washes. The sky is so fucking blue here. I feel so blessed by the silence and magnitude of desert sounds and southwest colors. The staccato of beautiful cactus wrens, hummingbirds, grackles, owls, and hawks. A ground squirrel approaches me. Somehow, she knows I will share my apple. There is some deeper meaning to this. A definite connection with a higher power. People on the trail miss out. I am suddenly sad for them.

"The earth laughs in flowers." - Ralph Waldo Emerson

Spending time in the desert, on the mountain, always rises above and beyond my expectations. Here, I am untamed, undefeated, and unafraid of anything. I am not anyone's wife, daughter, sister, mother, friend. Just me. The Sonoran Desert is my "right place" and my forever home. When Mother Nature shines upon me, I am free of all boundaries and burdens. There are no obstacles in my way. Yes, I can see clearly now. She and I have a mutual respect, a partnership for good. Her choice of barrenness teaches me everything that I need to know. She teaches me to respect and care for the natural world. I learn how to relate to what I see here, extremes and survival. I recognize my brightest light in the Valley of the Sun. What I think of my life is exactly what will come of it. It could never be clearer. If they can survive and thrive, I can do anything.

Karen Izzi, Phd

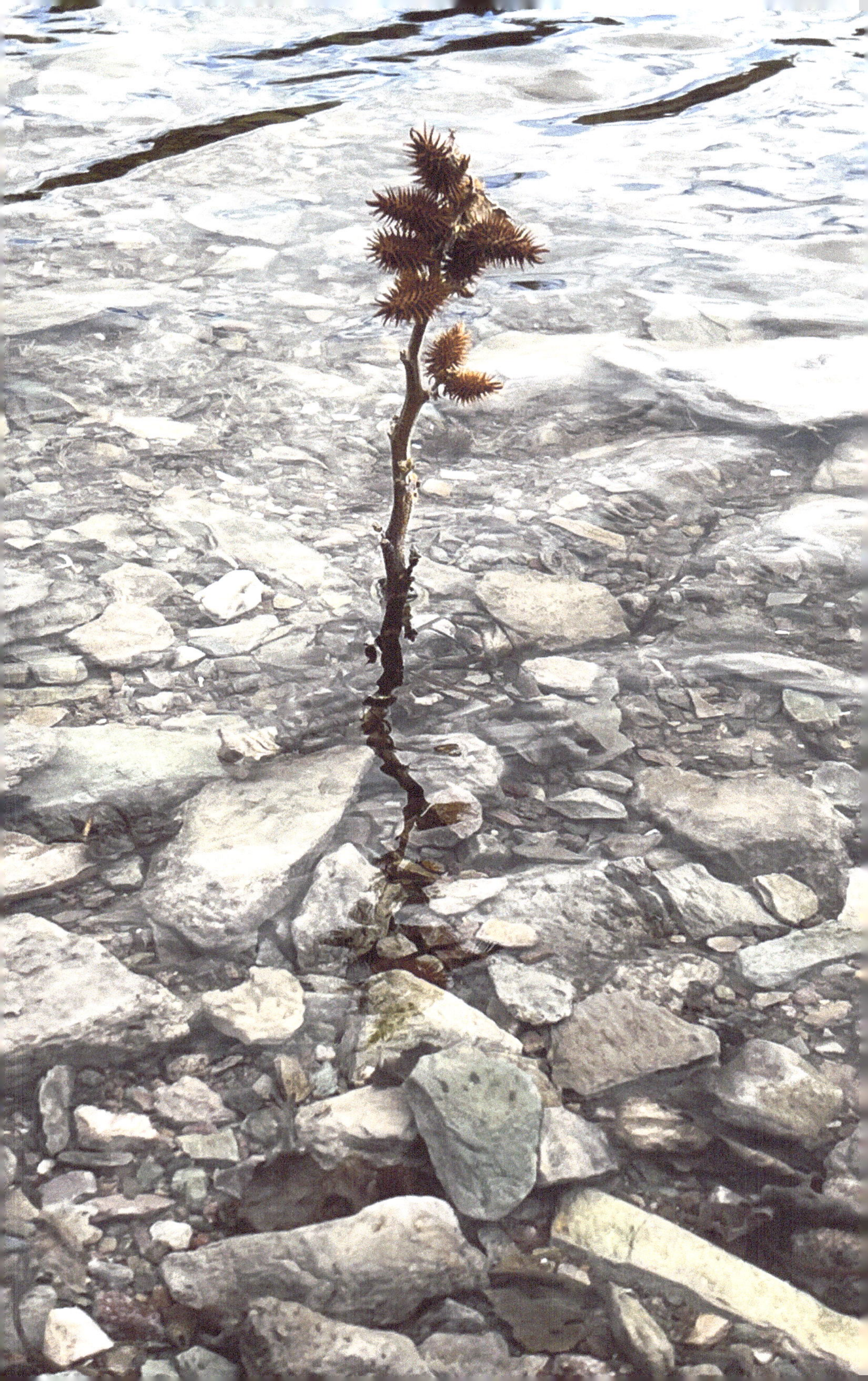

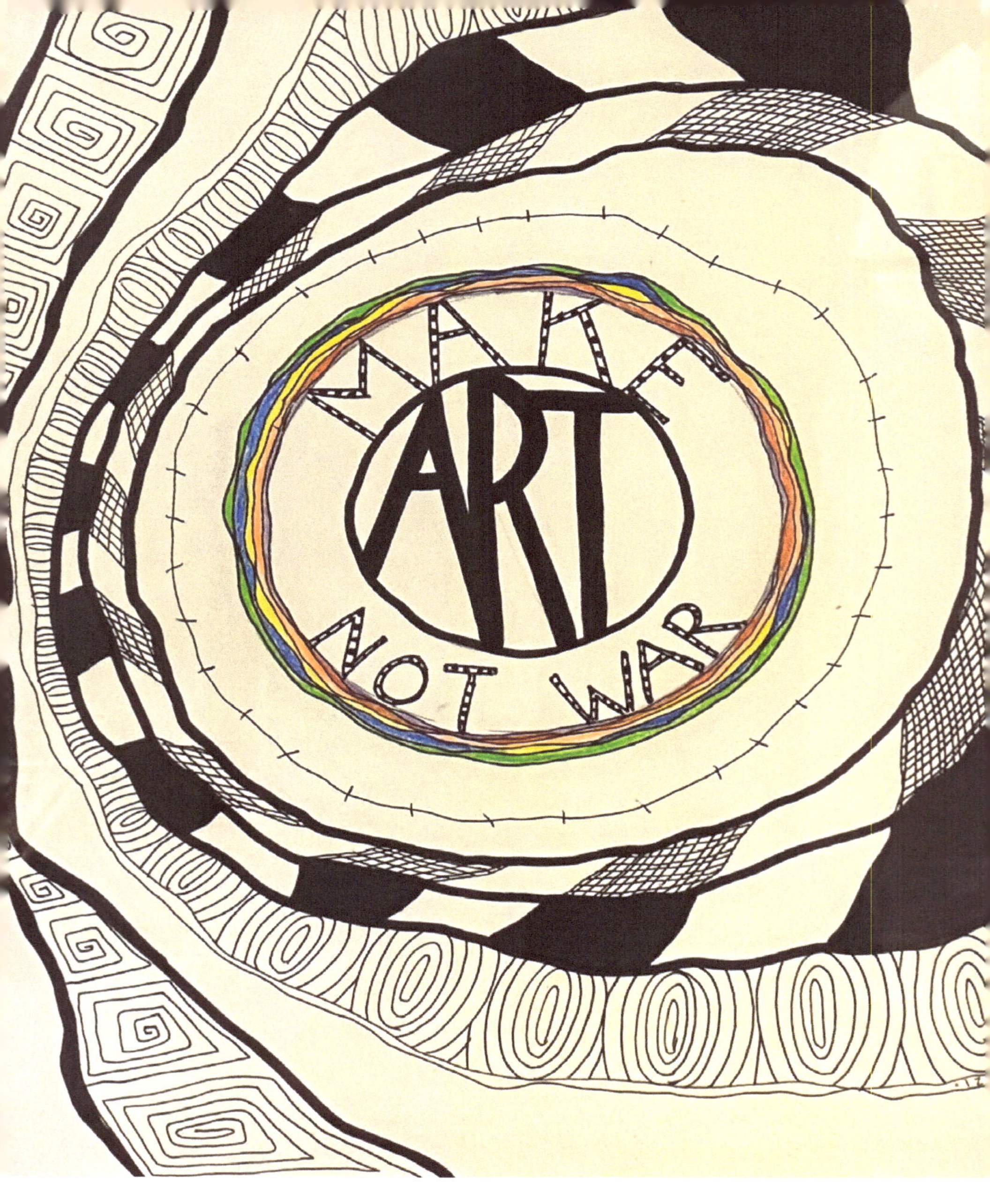

powerful words-this day.
i journey toward a new opening.
i offer my authentic self

an open invitation to grace

with ease,
                    i give of my heart.
                    i write.
                    i paint.
                    i draw.
                    i stitch,
not out of obligation, but to express my story,
i relax and release all that doesn't serve me.
things change. people change.
the universe pushes and moves me.
i am a well of life.
all the days that i live
i must speak to be free.
i have decided to tell a new story
with an ending i would be proud of.
i am not small anymore.
my path teaches me
that i can use my art, my words
for good, only good.
                    i write, i learn.
                    i paint, i forgive.
                    i tangle, i grow.
                    i sew, i feel healed.

                    i am open to learn,
                    breathe
                    and love.

                    there is only

                    love.

truth tellers

with wheel chairs and walkers
the visitors come
to escape monotony
one by one.

anything sacred
is private no more
their hearts are emptied
as they walk through the door.

———

more distant horizons
changing of meds
a hug from the housekeeper
a slight push from their bed.

with each hair swept
piles of dreams left behind
the pieces of them
stuck in my mind

after they've gone
i sit and smile
consider my own truth
and add it to the pile.

all aspects of their lives
husbands, seconds,
and third abandoned
by their children,
their voices
unheard.

little blessings

when he held my hand
i knew he felt happy
and when he squeezed my hand
i knew it meant
that he loved me.

always secure
in my grandfather's hand
wherever we went -
we took turns squeezing.

in the kitchen, the garden
or walking across the street
he taught me so much
about love.

i still hold his hand
and he still smiles
but now a tear forms
in the corner of his eye

little blessings
and the understanding
that no matter where we are
we will, forever feel
those little squeezes.

little scooch

no else knows me
like you know me.
how your finger zooms down my nose
or how i kiss you right in your ear.
until you push me away.

i've spent all the years of my life
getting to know you
and i hope we will spend
forever together -
me, your little scooch.

i pray for your good health
as you grow older
and thank god for your smile.
when i ask if you love me
you smile, just laugh, and say
"yeah, but not as much as tomorrow."

looking for emily

against my mother's wishes
i'm looking for my emily.
i wonder if she's the girl
in the car in front of me
who looked back several times.
is she the one in the magazine
with biceps that make me glance twice?
maybe she was the woman in the bookstore
asking for the feminist section,
or perhaps wrote the email that i received at lunchtime.

in poetry, i can create the perfect lover,
the one who fully dresses for halloween,
who loves to fight with whipped cream,
the one with her arms all around me
when we are out.
perhaps she wears her heart on her sleeve
and prepares a romantic dinner.
the woman who loves me -
loves my dog.

emily, wherever you are -
please, let me know it's you!

bronzed

i hear native spirit,
an imaginary flute,
and earthly drums in the distance.

spirit leads me to the barren land
where sunshine becomes my middle name.
my heart beats
to a warm, passionate, winter breeze.

mesquites of another lifetime,
i pass them
leaving only a dusty trail.

the mountain, delicate canvas
creating a new composite.
my heart listens and absorbs
the colors of the horizon.

for that one moment
as she wanders off,
i become the
sunshine
upon her
flushed
skin.

late one winter morning

i lay next to him
as he sleeps
watching the rise and fall
of his chest,
the lower lip pushing the top one
in a soft snore.

admiring his will to live
i try to sleep
as close to him as i can,
my hand comfortable
on his heart.
"keep going", i beg.

i revisit this morning's sermon.
over and over...
"we are *supposed* to offer thanks to god
for the person
and not dwell on the loss of them."

that's easy for her to say -
she doesn't know my grandfather.

mondays retreat

aunt mary sits in the front window
watching and waiting
for someone to visit -

a friend, her niece, or
just any familiar face.

on her bulletin board
i study her artwork, greeting cards,
special photographs,
and the bingo schedule -

she usually wins!

she touches my hand
and my own hectic life
suddenly retreats -

i breathe

others in the room
stroll in wheelchairs and walkers
as their lives mop up extra hours

they catnap or watch television
not noticing how special aunt mary is.
and she is...

in my father's heart

i am so mad at the president.
if he were my father -
i would like to die.

in my father's eyes
i sense calm,
the calm i seem to need.
in my father's heart
i appreciate gentle kindness,
the kind the whole world needs.

i see a bit of myself in him, too.
the witty, sarcastic side,
manifesting every last ambition-
and-i have those bushy eyebrows...
i favor being near him,
always wanting him to be proud.

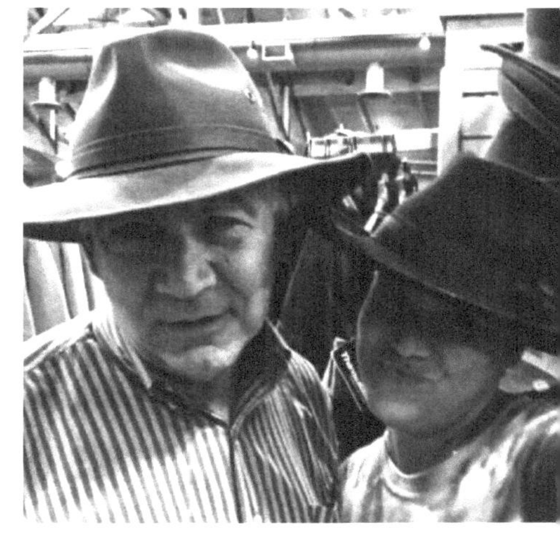

in his presence
i am myself -
we are one.
i want him to realize
that he is a better father
than anyone -
even his own father.

he is my ship to safety,
the mountain in my horizon
and my sun on the brightest,
hottest day.

i want him to grow
to be strong,
knowing that he is valuable
in more ways
than he will ever know.

we have all been waiting for
"the words"
and we still anticipate hearing
them, maybe at the end-

today,
i just choose to know
he loves me.

no babies

pale yellow cotton tee
and a string of wooden beads
temporarily take the place
of my lips on your neck.

tonight your smile still echoes
this morning's quiet
as you read and write
whatever your soul empties out.

beneath the table
your leg gently rests against mine
because you seem the need
to touch me.

the moon in its crescent form
shines light
on the other cafe guests
as they fade from our consciousness.

without children
me become who we are.

passion in the end

great-grandmom is 99 now
and our sunday visits continue to amaze me.

"they treata' me lika queen", she said.
"maybe i'a stay here for da resta' my life."

sometimes she goes down the hall -
when the nurse takes her.

"thosa gilrs take'a me wherever i wanta to go-"

so, she gets dressed every morning
and goes down o'the street" to the diner
where she has her own little table -
a place where she and her friends
all gather.

(tomar i'a go to da footballa game
and'a i watcha dos eagles win.)

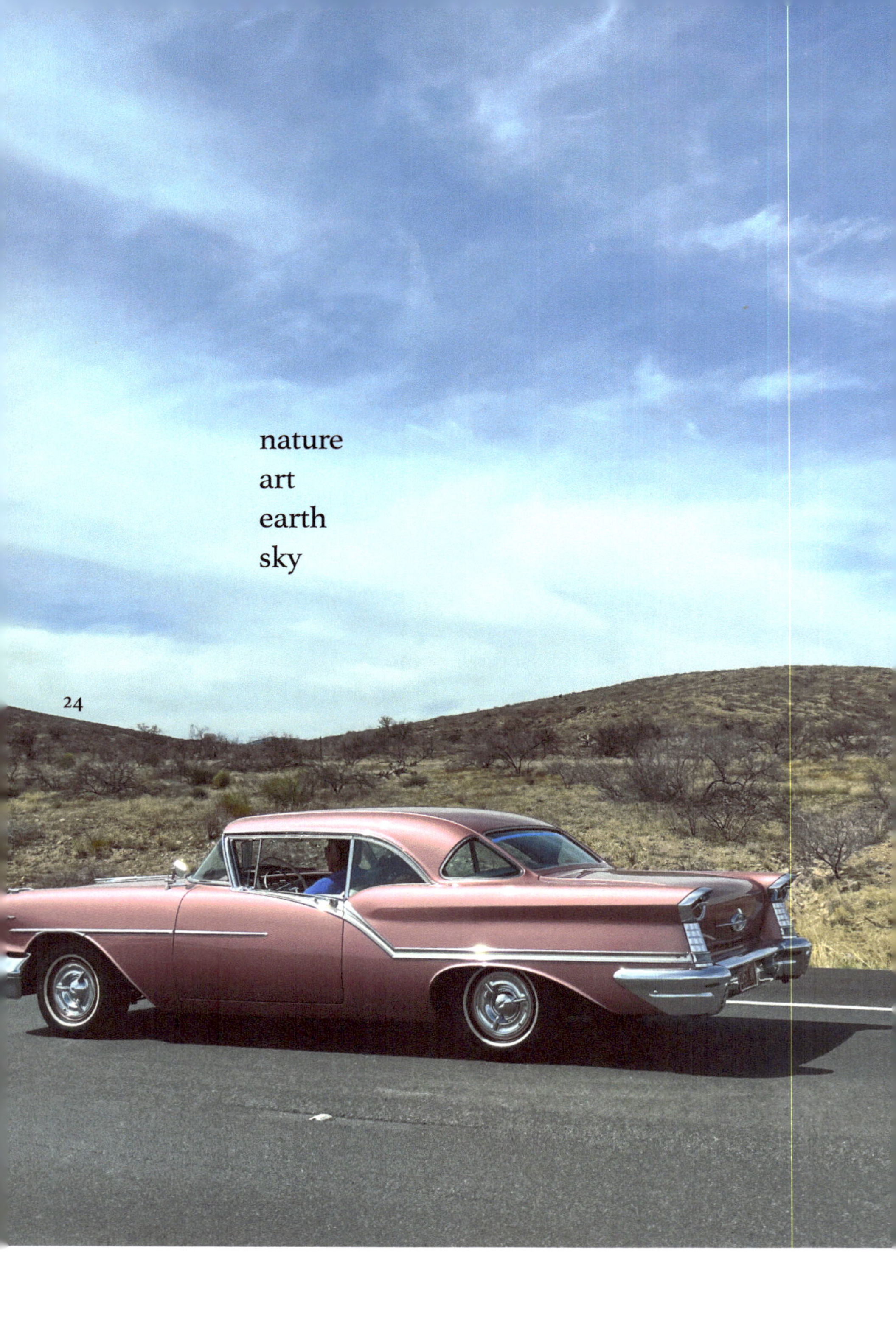

nature
art
earth
sky

everything sacred

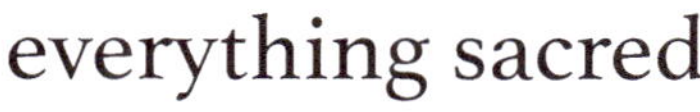

mesquite limb intersects
the peaceful blue,
desert sky warms my soul.
summery sun reflects itself
onto a nearby river
my spirit uplifted.
so deliberately the colors exist
blending nature, art, earth and sky.

i know
god thoughtfully
designed

        this day
        for the pleasure
        of
        my being.

pile of sticks

quite a collection
of sticks
i possess
in the short time
i've been here

some of the sticks
are perfect
others are broken,
odd, crooked and dull

they remain a token
of time
and represent reason

i learn much
from my sticks
about growth and change,
about being flawed and twisted

with my pile of sticks
i am sympathetic
suffering slight imperfections.

silver locket

does mom rcalize
the heart locket she gave me
at sweet sixteen
is still empty?

polished sterling
waiting to be filled
with a lover's lock of hair
or a minuscule photo
that will barely be seen.

it's ok dad has never said
those three little words
but if he wrote them in tiny letters
i could fold it up
and tuck it into my heart.

for now,
my locket echoes
"empty."

sparrow

from 11th street
in new york city
the sparrow writes...

he steals books
from the library
where he works -
hoping that someday
people will visit him
instead.

he sent me a photo
of a girl and a goat
in black and white.

the sparrow suggests
that we pray and sing
the same -
whether we are man,
woman, black, or white.

the sparrow has a fortune
in good lines -
a birthday sometime
in october
and a daughter
who loves
chinese food.

the marks of romance

i wonder if he told her
just how the roses in her garden
disappeared?

did he mention
the nights
we had spent at the piano
making beautiful
music?

did she even notice
that her laundry
had been folded
or the dog fed?

didn't she ever
drive by the playground
and see our swing?

i wonder if he ever told her
that he loved
me?

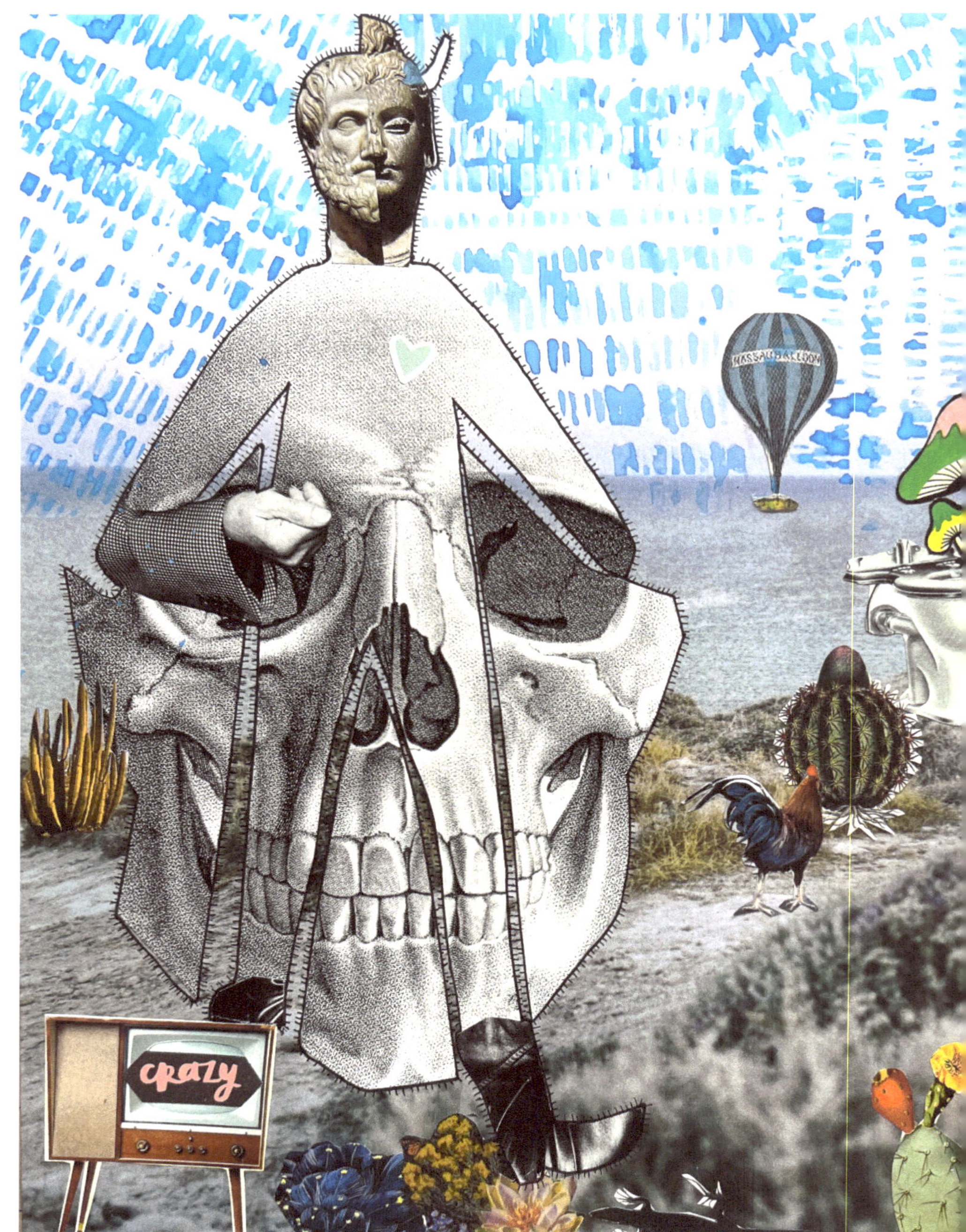
crazy

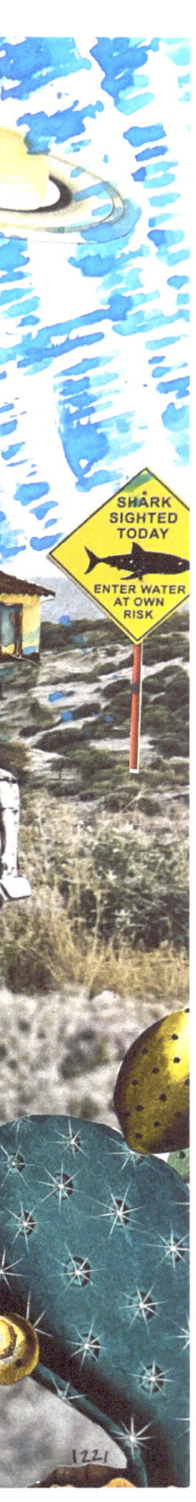

personhood

i have just stumbled over balance
and harmony
on the way to my bedroom

i will not sleep tonight
high spirits have returned to me
and I lay fidgety
like a small child
on christmas eve

i am not afraid
to see the intimacy
of time and silence
lay beside me

i can invent each new dream
with my own singularity
and uniqueness

this pleasure of solitude
written in the sky
is right outside my window.

the poem under his mat

the piano he plays
with such wisdom and
grace

a wave of sourds
swirl through her mind

as she watches,
her face smiles
lashes shutter
and her heart skips beat

through music
he whispers love
wishes on stars
spontaneously dances
and with music
they gather dreams

they spend years
staying the same
waiting for the next song

her ears wanting more

the plant people

i find that plant people are nice.
flowers and plants offer
something gentle to the world.
we recognize that.

i look up as i dig fearlessly,
with a prayer for the sun.
i reach both my hands into the earth
feeling the breath of the soil.

seeds sprout. i grow. flowers boom.
fruit appears.
i become a better person.
oh, the things
i've learned from a tiny seed.

people who plant things
are different.
we laugh easier.
we smile like a fistful of flowers.
we listen to the wind
and soak up the rain.

flowers don't carry their burdens.
they raise up with each ray of the sun.
they continue to sprout, bloom, and blossom
even when it seems impossible.

they keep watch over us
as long as they live.
the people who plant things
are happy.

the presence of god

it matters not that this man
is shaped like a beach ball

or that his arms rest
on the shelf above his belt

he opens the prayer booklet
to share with us
the presence of god

we join hearts to offer our prayers
standing helplessly with our tears
our memories and red noses

a flutter of emotion
soothes our grief

his skin
pale
of exhaustion

now
he rests

three of his daughters on my left
and this thick, unfamiliar man on the right

with folded hands
we pray
in the presence of god

things change

stretching up
to her tip toes
she painted
big strokes of
the tall trees she knows.

shades of green and grey
remind her of the psycho boy
she met in the woods.

the earth beckoned them
to the forest floor.
many times
he pushed himself
inside her.

engulphed in shades of green.
in one swift motion
she wrapped her arms
all the way around
his body lean.

she wants nothing more
then to have him here.
but he's left his body now
left the planet, disappeared.

tall trees on the wall.
she stares back
from her bed.
this time
just the memories
streaming through her head.

their energy
in motion
the gestures have become a blur.

through the forest they ran
high as kites
with their arms waving air.
they laughed till their faces hurt,
held hands
as wounded hearts repair.

timbers, toast & tamales

for two decades
and almost a half
i have abided.
no coffee i'd have
i've decided.
never once
i've not loved trees
the shade's protection
or raking of leaves.
the toast ma made
never did cool,
for pops buttered knife
his finest tool.
i've seized the glory
in each new day
in fact, learned happiness
and tamales the right way.

with this ring

how many diapers has the ring seen?
four children and eight grandchildren later,
i wonder this from time to time.

how much spaghetti dough,
how many apple pie crusts,
and how many bushels of tomatoes
must have slipped through her fingers?

with this ring my grandfather
promised his life to her
back in 1939 .
"from this day on"

on my finger now
i cherish and admire
the love that will last
a lifetime.

no one knows i wear it
except she and i.

this afternoon
we sob together
as he passes on.

i am left with the ring -
the priceless token
of a most wonderful bond -

i want to go back

i met a little boy leaning on the fence

he told me you miss me
said you're feeling lonely
and need to kiss me.

i want to fly
to let love soar
my heart in knots
he heard it roar.

i've been away too long
life's too short
he says i'm not wrong

thinking of you is all i do
each day and night
to get me through.

nothing in this world is safe
and nothing secure
so i want to go back
of that i'm sure.

oh, little boy, don't just stare
please, please tell me
when will i be there?

infectious smile

went to an art show
     a stranger smiled at me

a dark brown cow
fell off the wall
crashing onto the floor
at our feet
     nervous - we laughed

i had not dressed
to meet an artist
but he smiled anyway
     as wine dripped
     from the crack in his glass

an infectious smile
spread over me
just as a disease would
     taking over any effort
     i may have been making
     to seem uninterested
we sat on a bench to talk

we spoke of art
and suddenly he kissed me
     gently
passionately
     he smiled

not listening
i tried not to seem rude
but my thoughts were of
     how i'd please him

just ask her

she rumbles through the trash
to see what she can find
like a string saver
with one thing on her mind

you never know what she'll save
on a day like today
it may be the dreams we once gave

she gathers them together
for a collection in her fist,
notes from old friends and
the boys i have kissed

in the hands of a stranger
my memories will be kept
like my broken heart
or the tears we have wept

in those hands of hers
she holds all time
if you ever wonder,
this one is mine

her angel

retreating to the cozy chair
by the window,
i take the call.

so easily i surrender
to that certain sound,
the voice of an angel.

so many times
thoughts of her
flutter through my mind.
memories of her body
cause a pleasurable shiver
on a winter day.

i warm up to the possibihty
of loving the one i so adore.
in my quiet,
i am unable to comprehend
why we remain

———————————————— separate.

i sit withering,
begging for something
to fill the empty space
in my heart.

abstract

easel ready.
palette prepared.
i am a tired woman.
tired of the bullshit
the disrespect of people.

i stand up straight as my thoughts
greet unmarked canvas.
this can not go on.
colors separating
like oil and water
they become a wash
of misunderstandings and hate.

each of us
a creation to be seen
to be heard
to be loved.
fantasy on white.
generations splattered,
choked out and shot down.
blood stained and bruised.

my brushes are loaded.
drenched with color.
all colors.
i am ready
to create,
to paint the world with love.

i am a tired woman.
i will not contribute to the mess
that we have become.
this can not go on.

head noise in the notheast

this morning my interaction with the fog seems difficult.
i don't mean to have my head down.
but i am forced to watch my step, as i go on.
my mind is developing insufficient questions.
as i move along the wooded path,
i'm listening to the birds and
the noise in my head misbehaving.
the moment i stumble, the forest shouts out
"it'll be alright. catch your breath."

is there anyone else out here?
did anyone hear that?

i want to feel better
and be energized
and be more like my authentic self.
fucking fog is deeper and thicker than you can imagine.
the winter air is moist, heavy, and humid,
there's nothing but eeriness in my unsettled heart.
i cannot see the horizon, but i can hear the birds.
they act as if it's spring here. i know the truth.
they make every attempt to tell me.
"watch out for mother nature and take her by the hand.
it's your turn to guide her."

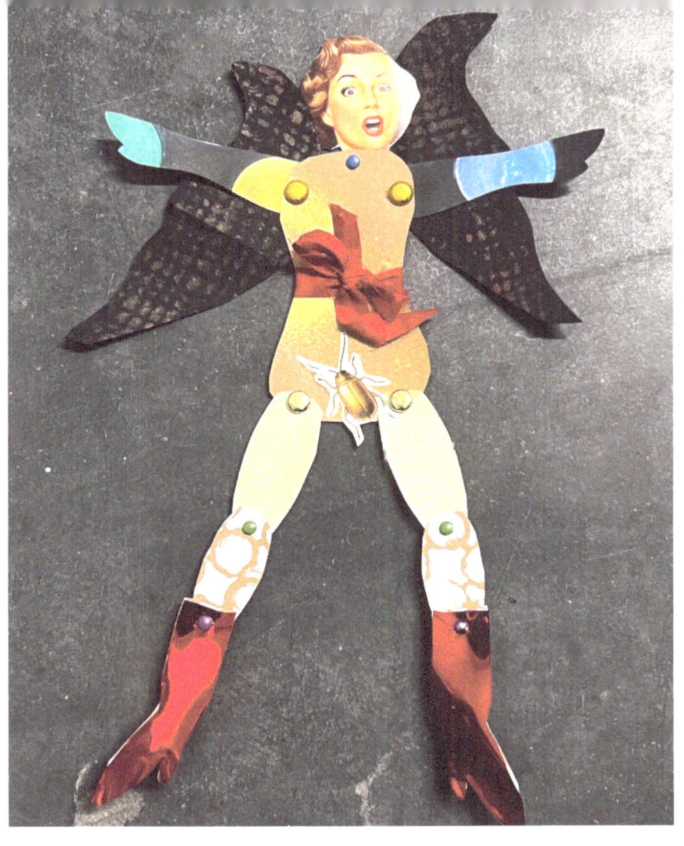

there is no witness.
this is all i know.
the atmosphere is thick. the sky is dark gray.
my thoughts come and go fast,
teetering back and forth
between being positive that the fog will clear
and feeling that my world is ending.
in this moment i know that i'm getting back on track.
living, breathing through the fog.
weakness gives way to a repetitive newsflash -
nothing stands in my way, but myself.

i just need a plan to get out of here.

care receiver

couldn't wait to sit in the sun
and write -

to explain how it feels
to have her tears
all over my face.

once a stranger
sitting across the table,
now my friend.

doesn't she know-
we each have fears,
darkness and doubt.

we all discard the pain
and hold on to the desire
to love again.

i let the sun
dry her tears
there on my face-
where she left them.

her open heart
let me in.

compatible

i enjoy listening
to her stories
being told from the heart

something in her
is such a big part
of me

her kisses
and welcoming hugs
always there for me

i reach
to breathe
her breath

resting my head
upon grandmothers breast

me
so much of her

mind on the water

i always walk curiously
like an explorer,
along the edge.

        the wind carries
        whatever the tide washes in
        toward me.
        noticing the waves
        moving back and forth,
        i lose my balance.
        it reminds me of the necessary motions
        that i make to get me through the day.

      the wind carries
      my merciless thoughts
      silently, thank god,
      powerfully
      to their end.

someone knew
that this is just what I needed
this morning.

the wind brings
thick clouds
to cover blue sky.
rain begins
to pound my face.
heavy drops
wash clean,
my spirit.

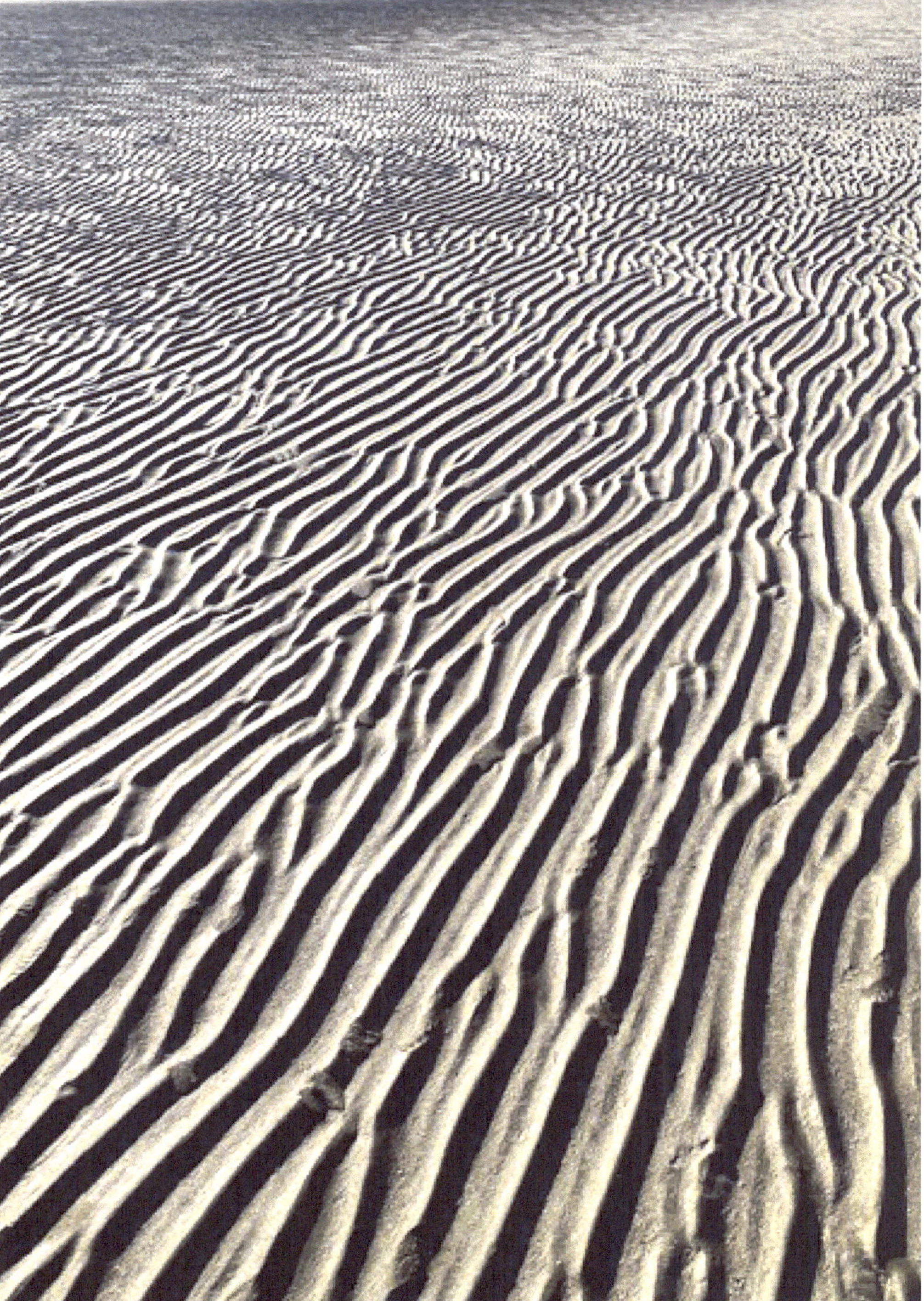

deception (self)

she doesn't realize
how many days passed -
days lost in the shuffle
of obtaining the perfect son.

she forgot to teach him
that love isn't always quiet
and that it is ok to tango
with simple excitement.

she forgot to tell him
it's ok to be strong
and meet others half way -

all right to take time
to dance inside
and explore the seed
growing within

i don't know how
she could have
forgotten.

he is strong,
independent -
with a voice
all his own.

he is bold,
joyful -
with a high place
in the world.

winter birds

if it's not
the old dime - gray sky
that brings them
and not the bathing dish
around back
not the leaf-abandoned magnolia
or the wood in its' neat stack

      it must be the absence of footprints
      across the snow-white ground
      or maybe the tiny seeds
      speckling your sidewalk
      which they have found

divine comfort

from the porch
an old woman
daydreaming of her lover
immerses herself
in the storm

wind howls
as the daisies
protect sidewalks close by

so many of her dreams
she still believes
though at times
difficult -

sun peeks through
darkest sky
letting it's light shine
off porch railing
into her eye

the sky
reaches down
interrupting the rain
and offers her a rainbow

everyone's famous

at the bookstore cafe
i notice a man
speaking very loudly
to his friend.

long mustache sipping coffee
the other sketching a space ship
they discussed new york
politics and what a jewish jerk
barbara streisand has become
as they both colored in the lines.

i consider the spaceship,
the basis of their opinions and
laugh out loud as i notice
their little girl pencil case,
and alien erasers
spread out across the table.

minutes later
i realize, in my ignorance,
that they might be
someone famous.

oak creek canyon

the forest calls me closer
i look up at the red rock
knowing in my heart
i want to stand up there-
at the very top
and suck in the view.
all of my senses
suddenly awakened.
broken down leaves
crunch beneath my steps.
i pause to look up
and photograph trees
against the bluest sky.
with a million colors-
i lose count
of how many combinations
appear right before my eyes.
one leaf, with its nine colors,
catches me
just before i step forward.
this moment in time
just us -
on fire.
it's a custom blend.
a miracle of a leaf
has blessed my day.
voices of kids laughing
and exploring
interrupt my gaze.
i hike on
approaching the mountain side.
in the forest the trees listen -
they never judge.

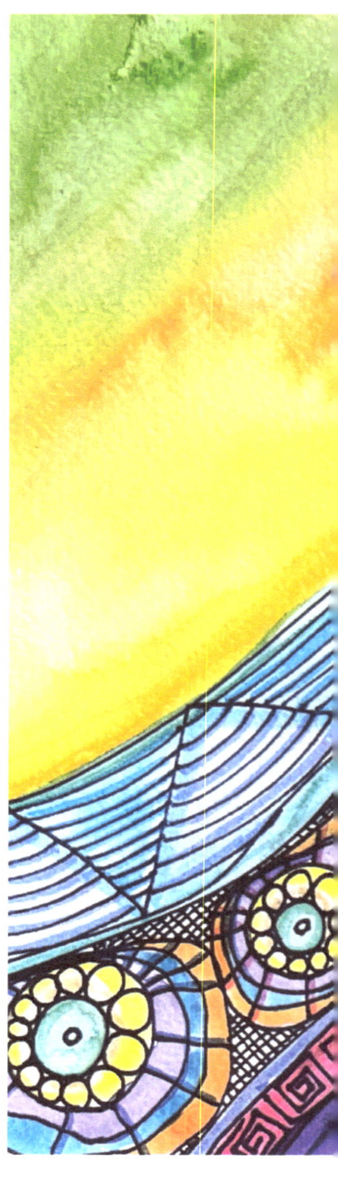

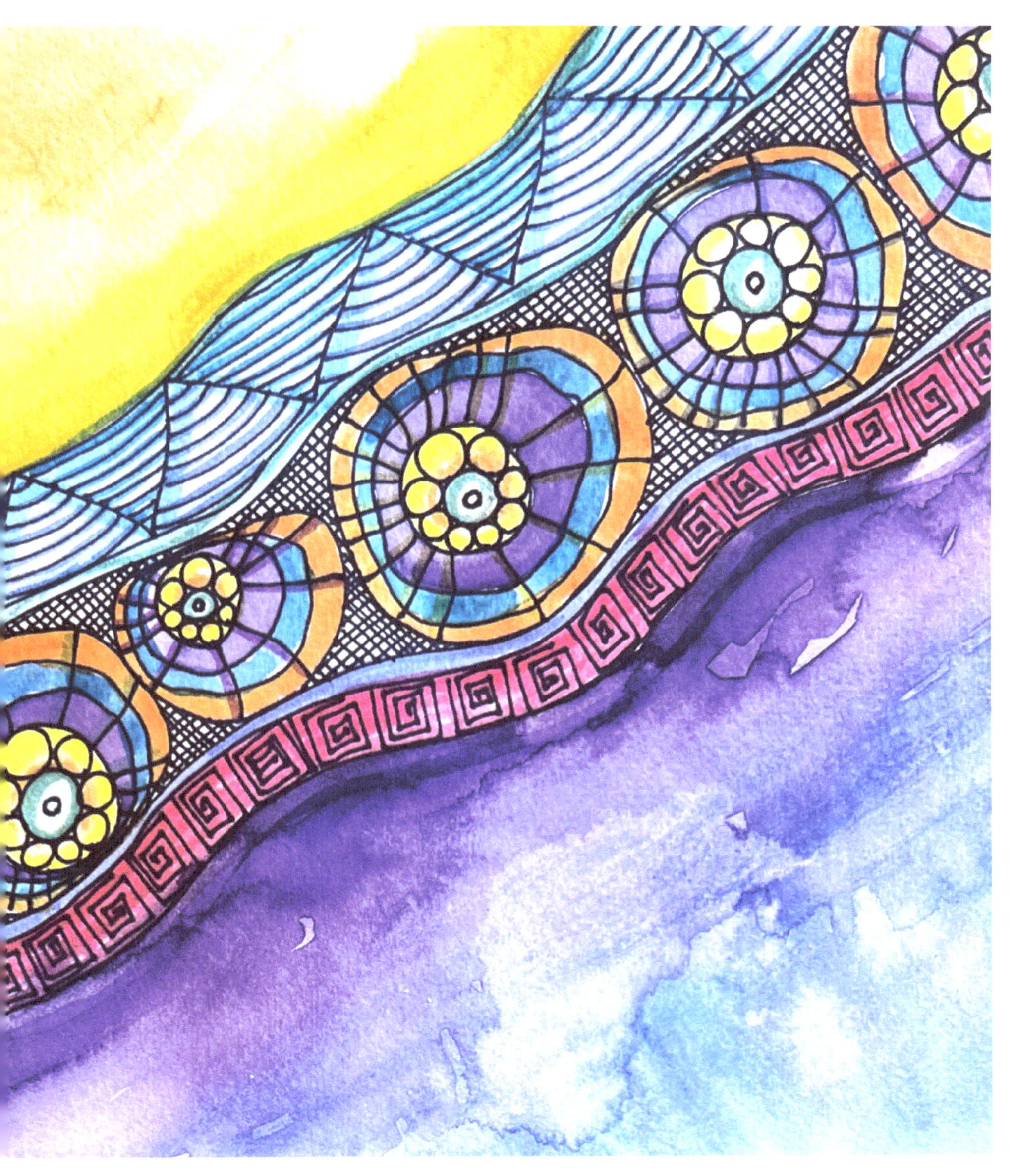

they simply sway
back and forth
standing tall
providing emotional shelter,
listening to my thoughts.

flash back

adelina,
sleeping in your room
brings me right back
to being sixteen, like you.

"ooh la la"
sexy photos
of famous boys,
bits of makeup.
pink slippers, hats and journals ...

medals for flips and bends
remind me
that everyone is good
at something.

days full of hours on the phone
so many wishes, wants and desires
a collage holding up the wall.

secret smiles hidden away
tears, smiles and tears again.
bicker with mom,
extra hugs to dad
to stay up later or
to talk just a little longer.

once upon a time
and happily ever afrer
all happens so fast -

makes it impossible to sleep.

first marriage

every once in a while
i google his name.
i look online
just to see what he looks like now,
a peek at what his life might be like

i imagine he is well.
how we see the world
used to be the same
but how we moved forward
is still in question.
we didn't stay to work it out.

———————————————

i am accountable for
my actions
my choices
my ideas
and i've learned to cope
thirty-three years later,
with his.

faith keeps me going,
knowing,
visualizations
heal
and cause me to grow

we move in so many directions
to sanctify our space
only allowing
the light to penetrate
the cracks,
the gaping holes
we have had for ages.

i am open now, to receive
all the good
that the universe has for me
and for him.

the world is spilling over
with goodness.
we were just young
stubborn
and exploring
different things.

treasure

you seem so isolated
and forgotten
a treasure washed
to shore

your scalloped edges
caught my eye
and i followed you -
deposited
just under foot

after many years
of bashing against
the sand
you must be so worn
all of that rolling
and endlessly spinning

i look inside
to see
just as far as i can
what treasures do you hide,
how did you make it here

to find

me?

raging rain

perched on the edge
of this simple brook
in the shade
nature surrounds me
where rabbits tell stories
and coyotes sing for free
i notice something bizarre
sounds like war and
silence no longer exists
the clouds are bickering
tossing their broken lines
across the sky
i sense your presence
my blood runs hot
and my heart flutters
then it stops
in the middle of nowhere
the mist of freshwater
brought by the wind
somehow cleanses my soul
come, i shall show you this paradise
i call rain

no boundaries

protected by endless blue sky
i bask
in the afternoon sun.

a blackbird
bustles and romps
chasing scattered crumbs
another one left behind.
the ice cream man
performs his jingle
up and down the dirt roads -
reluctantly, i pause to listen.
a fly lands briefly
to suck the moisture
from my skin -
i let him tickle me.

rainbow trail -
just passed the middle of nowhere
is where the sun seduces me
and the southwest wind
refreshes my mind.

i want nothing more
than to live
then
die here.

white

with a flicker of white
for ease i flee
the wind blows cold
survival is up to me

a cardinal session on the frozen slopes
nourishment nowhere to be found
a yard full of seed
we must be blind

i lounge nowhere
but on chimney tops
catching the warmth
before it stops

serrated, icy thorns hang
crystal clear
melting by the second
the spring must be near

my feet shackled
beneath this lifeless bed
i hop, i run
to get away
from this crunch of white
i no longer wish to tread.

rainy day

where this mood came from
i don't know.
maybe the swollen creek
outside the library window,
rushing furiously into the lawn.

my body is wired,
hungry for springtime energy.
my mind won't rest
i struggle with the conflicts,
cravings, anger, and delusion.

where might i find enlightenment?
in a flower, seed, or a newborn
or maybe in this quiet place.

my considerations:
i am alive
i am free
i have the power to feel.
i believe there are no accidents,
there are no failures

just a hell of a lot of rain.

sedona morning

top of the morning
bottom of the canyon
red rocks and magestic pines
naturally decorate
a walk along the creek.

crisscrossing over moving water
i take each step mindfully.
notice myself moving
with the flow,
gaining strength in each new grip
and each new footing i obtain.

i feel mysef, inside, grow stronger
purposefully healing
with each new breath
a pause to look around
where the colbalt sky
meets the greenest branch.

snap of the camera -
the only unnatural thing present,
breaks the silence
for a split second.

a new day,
red rocks
magestic pines
bottom of the canyon,
i secretly wish
i was lost.

118 degrees

i am earth infused, dirty, and indigenous
all natural.
i was born to be in the wild
both feet on the earth
nose in the air
face in the sun
hands in the soil.
i am fearless in the wash
blissfully ignorant and unstoppable
at the mountain.
i am refreshed, enlightened
and fully alive.
my mind is aligned with mother nature
cacti, birds, bees, and the trees.
i experience my life at every moment.
i am alive with infinite possibilities
among the tumbleweed
under the big blue sky.

hummingbirds challenge my attention span
while rocks remain unmoved for centuries.
nature as therapy
my breath
my beating heart
hot wind sweeps through this place.
i'm sitting still
listening for a long time.
i need not reply.
a direct hit from the universe
like a smack on the side of my head.
an immediate life changing
sustaining experience.

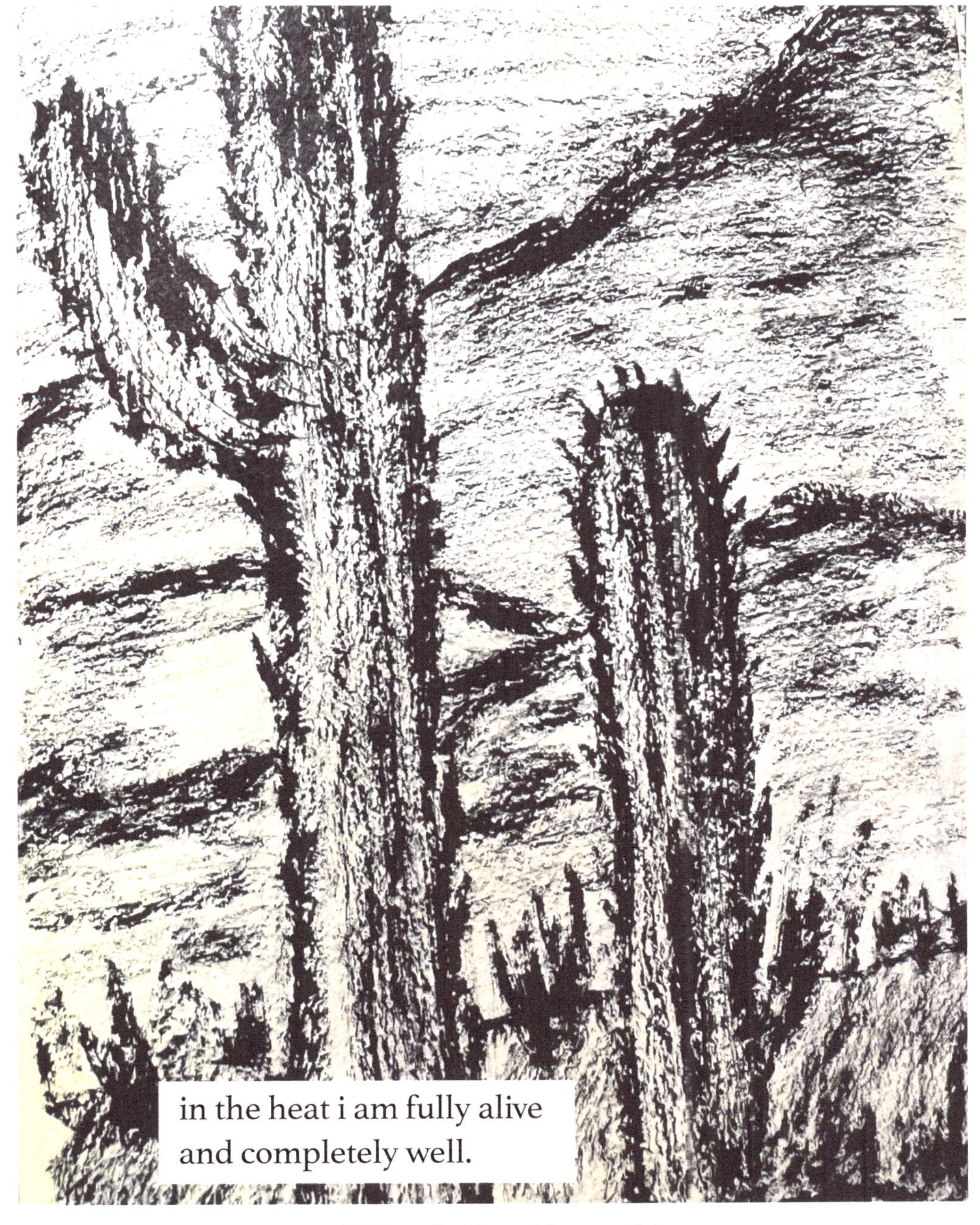

i am part of this whole wide world
enchanted at every moment.
my body and spirit requests this.
each day a new way of loving & living and learning.
i cultivate the magic of my view.
i'm learning how to live slow.

sleeping with the light on

rummaging through
all of these lines
i had rehearsed
how beautiful
the day had been
singing songs
dancing like children
in the sun
we tossed glimpses
just as the tunes
outside my screen
from where i lay
the birds sing
at all hours of the night

locomotion

vivid graffiti
you splurge
on the walls of my palace
a royal gem
infecting me
with a roar of satisfaction
you're bonded by excellence
and labeled by princely tracks
with a noble handshake

we promise
union until the end
may our existence
be as everlasting
as these tracks
that have carried you
to my palace

spring garden

this is a secret no one ever told me about.
something i never learned as a child.

something i found in my own backyard.
excitement rushes over me as crocus litter the lawn
and trees smile over paper whites.

red tulips glisten next to golden ones
and squirrels dig out their winter
treasures.

each day i
sit down with the earth

and as the sun sheds light
upon life

i
thank god

summer soltice

a dance through time -
swirling 'round
and 'round

making a new memory
never touching the ground.

ten fingers rigid -
and align with the sky

goddess of the moon
so full and high.

i skip along
the mountain ridge
laughing with a sigh

erasing
harmful patterns,
old scars and cry.

summer woods

i anticipate the smell
and mysterious sounds of the woods

tonight spring gives birth
to a whole new series of life

crickets ...
i sit up in bed-
or are they peepers that speak to me?

through the screened window
they invite me
to come out and play

but i am cozy in my bed i stay,
with my chin resting on my palms

balmy air makes its way
to morning dew.

that kind of day

it's where mountains meet the sky
the sun decides to rest.
under pinkish purple clouds
and soothing shades of blue
there are miles of trails to expose
and so much more of you to know.

in your absence i imagine your smile
and eyes facing the sun.
with your arms wrapped
all around me
i know you would catch
the same shapes
the clouds make.

the synchronicity of our breath...
let me stop here
to take a little rest -
like the mourtain
and its sun.

the wind

the wind
many times
our paths have crossed
you capture my eye
with dust
destruction
and disaster
but i enjoy
your tranquil moods
as you graze through my hair
the way you move
your elasticity surrounds me
you bustle against my face
glide over me
and stir beneath me
i hear you
whistle through the tree
outside my window
and so many times
hear you tap my roof
with the stars you fling

amazing grace

she joined a choir
led by god
we sing
our gods are the all the same

inspired voices
unite hearts and song

with pride we sing
together
we fight joyful tears
that flood our eyes

bodies overcome
with energy
emotion
goosebumped
and tickled –

this choir radiates
joyful praises
of our own

what agrees with me

i choose wide open spaces
clear sky - quiet morning
and mind.

i follow fate
hoping to be spared
all the shit
of the evildoers

i consider the continuation
of breath
the impossibility
of living a day
without thinking.

i sit up straight
and wait for the sun,
my only true source of strength
and inspiration.

winter morning

as the day begins
the horizon doesn't seem freaked out at all
about losing its rich golden glow.

birds soar overhead
as i rush through leaves
struggling to get to just the right spot
for my camera's morning snap.

ready for new adventures
i study the tree lined sky.
brightest orange to pale,
pale yellow,
i admire the gradual turning to blue.

chilly air forces its way through me.
i catch my breath and
cleanse my lungs.

i pause
as the sun makes its debut
on this new day.

plane ride home

the candle burned
all the way out
as we made love

we didn't even notice
the darkness
as it set upon us

for days
it was the two of us
sharing ourselves
soulfully,
respectfully

we smiled
and smiled again
holding our hearts together
promising nothing more
than to remember

now as i watch you
standing in the window
to wave goodbye
i realize
that never before
have i cried
this hard.

wind in my face

the wind against my face
reminds me of the resistance
that some people have
to happiness.

my happiness.

the blue sky isn't
enough for them
they will need an accident
or something larger,
like death -
divorce or not enough food -

then it's much too late
for them to realize.

they should have been happy
with the wind in their face.

worth going on sunday

i listen to the reverend
so prepared and confident with speech.
i crisscross my legs, noticing each vein.
i pick at lose cuticles
as my thoughts wander
far from the sermon.

water trickles from the fountain
i consider my laying awake
long after midnight last night
and what the full moon may have to do with it.

like a trek down the mountainside
the talk, an unconscious comprehension.
i fight the tear in my right eye
as it has a mind of its own.

i clutch the hand of my friend
admiring her cheekbones
and the spirit in her smile.
as she looks at me
from the corner of her own tear-filled eye

i suddenly believe in magic.
the magic of the moment.
in the purpose of love.
the moment of now.

transformative embrace

i have fallen quite smitten
with the vulnerability and
passion i feel for this place.

my life is new in the garden.
i am a connoisseur of evolution,
mountain soil, blue sky,
and the soul of the earth.

my core has healed itself here,
in this place.
i dream the future
indestructible.

i ache for the idea
of changing the planet,
striving that we live consciously,
without poisoning the earth.

i pursue all possibilities.
i imagine deeply,
and am reborn.
magic forms.
creamy yellow winter roses bloom.

a thousand sunsets

time to leave my worthlessness behind
all things unfinished
dark selves and insecurities

when i am quiet
you are swarrn of bees
a steady buzz in my ear
provoking me to listen

helping me realize the sweetness
of my own heart
my confidence returns
inspiring it, poetry, pure love

in a thousand sunsets
i have wished for you
keeper of the bees
protector of my heart

my new existence knows
self respect
and deepest love
because of you

jeep

sahara-like heat and wind batter
my eyes. my hair will be a disaster.

we talk about sex and the weather
as he drives and i watch the desert
pass us by.

i try to decide what it is that makes
me think of moving out here. my
life is at home in my house and
luscious green garden.

here, the cactus are still in the same
places i left them - years ago, with
their dehydrated arms waving out
and birds pecking and resting on them.
nothing green grows here, i
convince myself, except these
cactus.

i imagine how strong they must be -
to survive - and thrive. each spring
they bloom - wonderful flowers.
how can they grow only one inch
per year and still stand so firmly to
protect their space?

he looked over at me, keeping his
eye on the road, and smiled. once
again he looked over to ask me
what i was thinking...
———————————————— i could only say,
"saguaro".

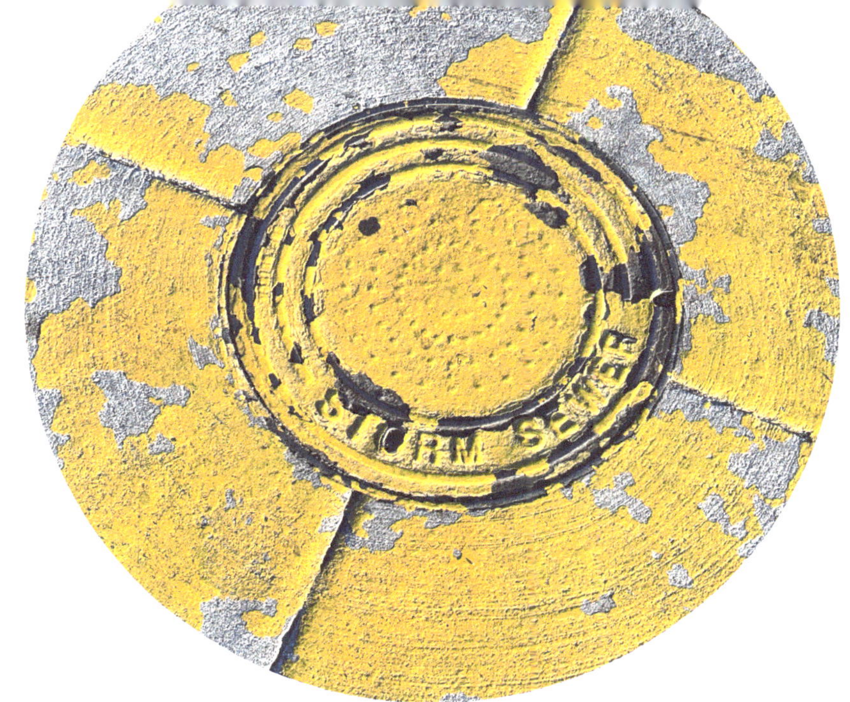

hole in the moon

naked
in midnight black -
a full moon

tonight -
our motions
collide and flutter
through the air

high
in frolic -
i swallowed
a mouthful of sky

maybe
superhuman pleasure -
with all my might
i put a hole in the moon

a vacant drain

curiously i stand over a vacant drain
no one stops to wonder if the water
is melted snow or maybe just rain

the cinders and old boot prints
vanish before my eye
don't know what i will see here
as time passes by

a corner of a dollar bill
a mint's wrapper and this moment
all lost among the slush

my stare lasts but a minute
as the current devours them whole
i will kiss them goodbye
when i continue my stroll

somewhere far away they will end up
in someone else's drain
hours after i am gone

will they even notice?

afternoon showers

two homeless dudes
smile and converse
as they look up to the sky
they get rained on

i slam the car door near them
thunder roars, lightening strikes my heart
and water pours passed me

millions of teenage dreams
now, middleage wishes
rushing right down the drain

two ex-husbands, no children
no house, no home
i am nobody
going nowhere

its not safe for me
to be outside
on a day like today
i want to strangle somebody

face to face

six squirrels call from the garden
skipping over abandoned deck chairs
still and lonely,
just as we left them in october.

to see what they can find,
they carefully pick through kindling
at the back door.

with twitching, wooly tails they
glimpse at me
and return to their search.

> they carry off sticks and leaves
> to their tall trees,
> making winter repairs.

i step out to provide them with breakfast,
face to face with the winter wind.

my steps do not interrupt them.

fall darkness

i ran through the night
to get here
barely breathing,
almost tripping

racing wind-blown leaves
around and around
empty space

dizzy, twirling,
simply swirling
crunches catch my fall

tonight darkness
is a treasure
tucked away
among the leaves

i've gotten so lost,
will i ever find
my way back home?

open window

inhale
and become intoxicated
by autumn air.
i remember the candlelight
and reimagine you all over me,

as leaves fall
they land
one on top of the other
like us becoming one.

remember our breathing
synchronizing hearts
and connecting spirit.

you warm me
inside and out
as you cradle
the back of my head
to pull me close.

inhale
i lay on your chest.
open window
beyond words.

racoon dance

the ring of fire is healing and warm
against my cold cheeks.
it flickers for us
in the winter air.
fire makes everything better.
it seems as if it's melted together.

in the haze
i see a racoon
peeking out of the evergreens.

now that the day
is full of darkness,
it watches us dance
and laugh around the flames.
beer bottles cling salute
and it runs to hide.

    they wait for next nightfall.

tomorrow
when maybe we won't see them.

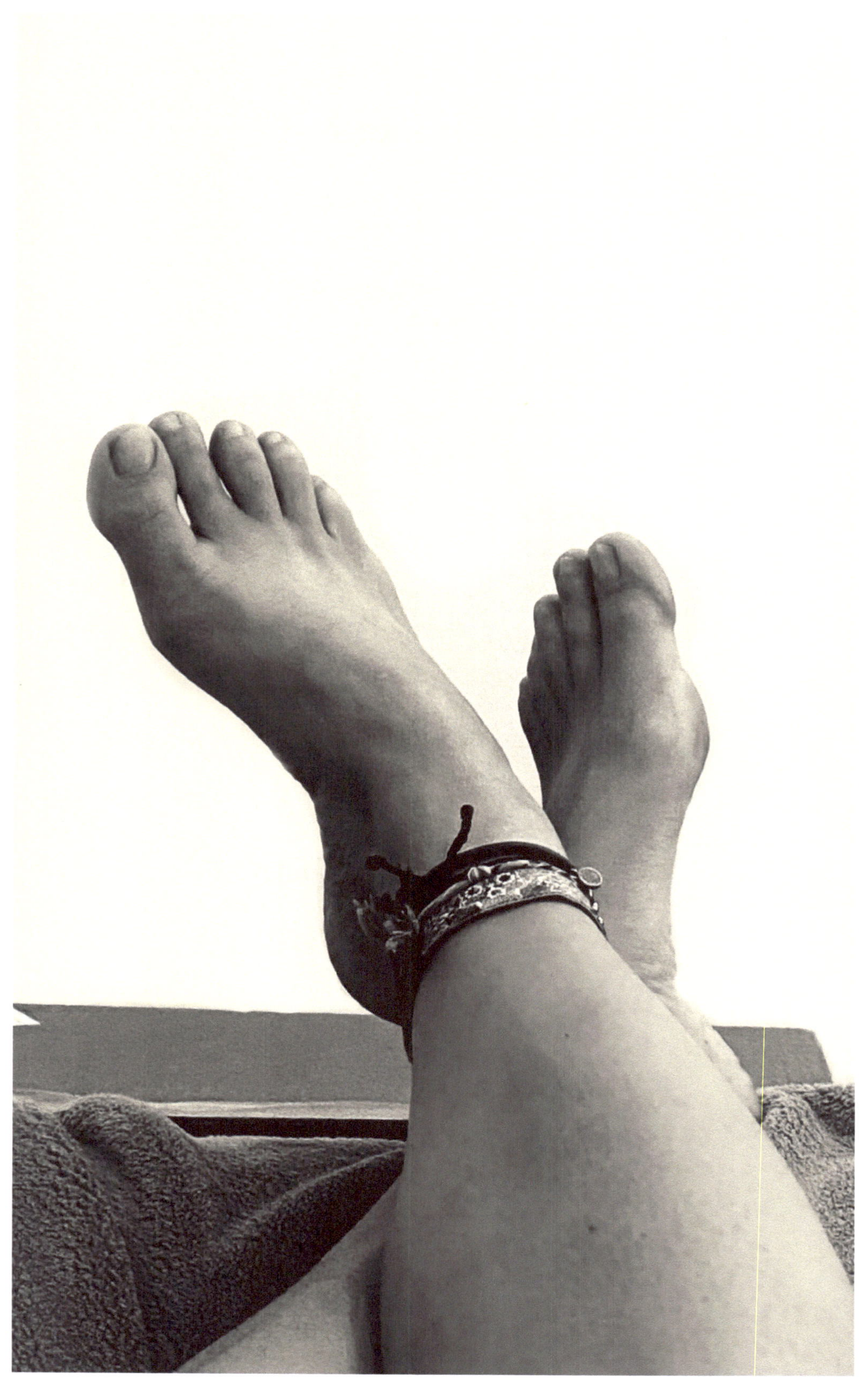

playmate

clothes clutter the floor.
sheets -
      cool mint green
the walls -
      bright.

the memory of this morning
      dances in
      bringing
      the summer breeze.

it was our own invitation
      to scatter
      our clothes
      across the floor -

      to lay our bodies
      face to face -
      a playground for the wind.

      this afternoon
      i recall
      your certain power
      to possess delight -

      just as the breeze.

just plain jane

loving you is a fight
tell me who i must be
to love you

when i hear her voice
i scream her name
in thoughts
and body

she makes me light up
remembering
where she placed
each and every kiss

i try to walk away
but i can't

loving you is a fight
i let you back in
but i'm not what you want

when i hear her voice
i want to run
to her
scream her name
she brings me to life again

and again

the rhythm of autumn

this morning's sun
is up before me.

while soft sounds create silence
and shapes make thoughts
on the wall,

i watch her breath
waiting
with excitement, for her to wake.

random strokes
i make on her chin
because i like the way it makes my hand feel
soft lips, she drifts from her dreams

just outside our window
leaves blow crazy
as our bodies move together.

the crack in the window
allows the breeze,
the rhythm of autumn,
and desire.

host of passion

i have not forgotten
the burning
desire
which led me to you

i didn't mean to fall in love
though
i know
you sensed the burning flame

life brings us love
and in love
i live,
the host
of your burning passion

two writers

with her hands in my hair
she said, we should write about this -
i remained kneeling above her
kissing her face.

        carefully i watch him
        touch me
        i with his eyes -
        soundless warmth seduces me.

my mind races my fingertips
my lips pressing her skin -
alive like a butterfly
landing weightless.

        he sits indian style now
        gracefully writing -
        thinking, writing
        wanting me again.

as she pauses beneath me
my heart longs for her -
without a word spoken
she reaches for me again

and again.

train ride

my heart is exhilarated
listening to her body

i feel her reach
for me
her lips as silk
cling

her wet mouth
re-hydrates me
after being apart

moments flash
like a trainride

    reminding me

    of how much

    i need to be

    in her presence

be patient

Be patient towards all that is unsolved in your heart and..
try to love the questions themselves like locked rooms
and like books that are written in a very foreign tongue.

Do not now seek the answers, which cannot be given you
because you would not be able to live them.

And the point is, to live everything.

Live the questions now.

Perhaps you will then gradually, without noticing it,
live along some distant day
into the answer.

- Rainer Maria Rilke

not concerned

my heart trips and stumbles.
i tell myself you can't get to me
anymore.
but the fire never burns all the way out.
it lights me up as
i continually toss myself into the flames.
i reimagine the way we were
a hundred times or more.
my delicate heart
your soft smile
idle mind,
my soul is all yours.
whose side am i on anyway?
i lie when i tell myself
i don't miss you.
hot flames make me unconscious
warped and infinite.
i stand here in a stupor
with the fire too close to my skin.

i want to fall into your arms
into the fire.
even as the window to the heart of me
shatters.
with the letting go
i crumble
again.

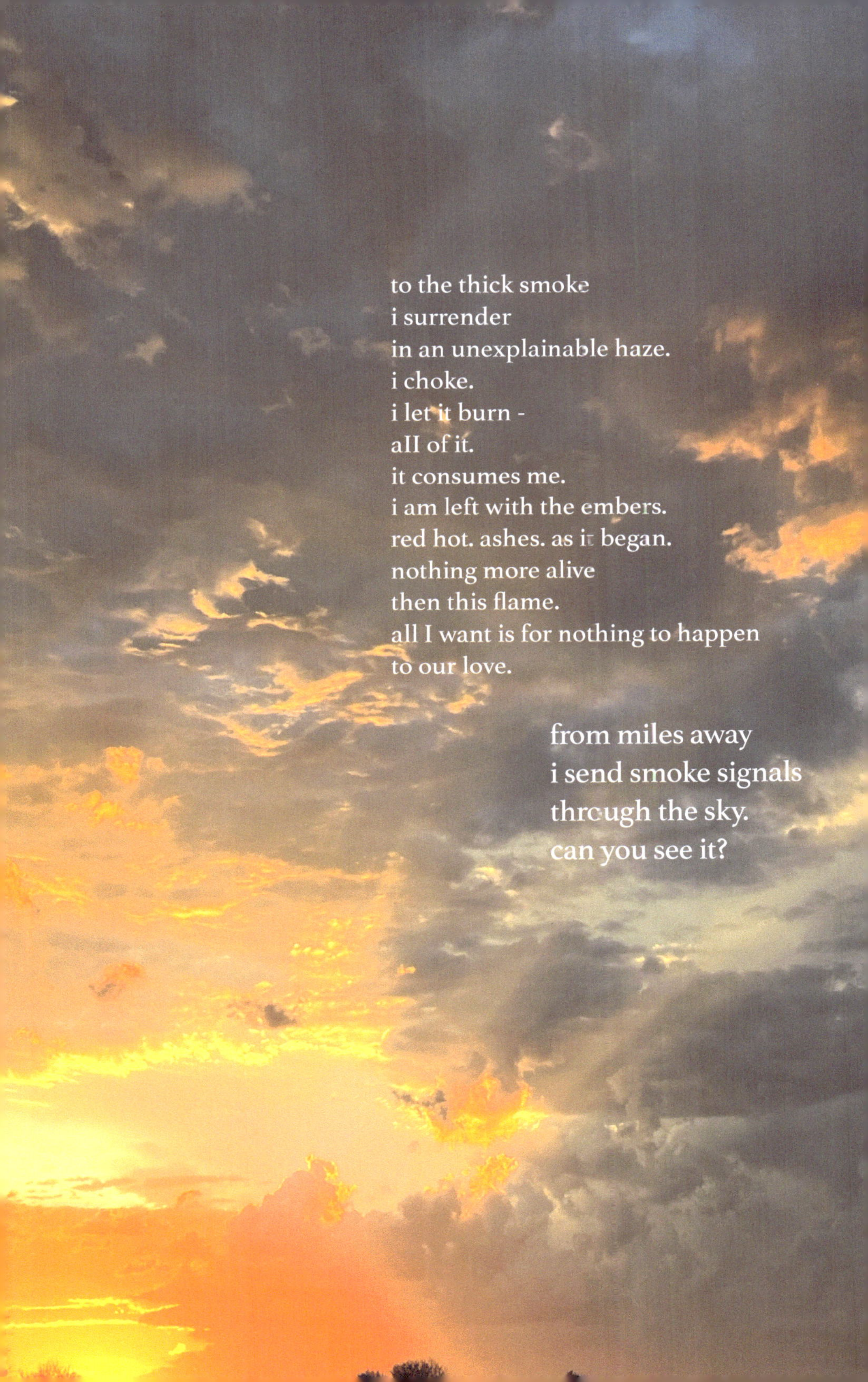

to the thick smoke
i surrender
in an unexplainable haze.
i choke.
i let it burn -
all of it.
it consumes me.
i am left with the embers.
red hot. ashes. as it began.
nothing more alive
then this flame.
all I want is for nothing to happen
to our love.

from miles away
i send smoke signals
through the sky.
can you see it?

passing the time

i cherish the moments
when i would watch you smile.
i recall orr closeness -
now reduced to memory.

i consider the time
in between
seeing the love in your eyes -
realizing the goodness in your heart.

so many hours
after i lay down to sleep
i pass the time -
listening to my heart speak

on the last day

she taught me to love
who i am

there are many reasons
i believe her

she's romantic,
energetic
and magical

i'm not gonna worry
about how much i love her

it's a fine feeling
and will never
escape me

slowly unfolding

all of the rules i've learned
are broken,
now
into my face
the wind took her hair

i try and catch my breath
after seeing her
once again
and into my face
the wind took her hair

i kissed her
just as i've always wanted
almost losing my breath
when into my face
the wind took her hair

    slowly
    we unfold

stepping back

moving from the calm ocean
which brought me fresh salt air
in the early morning,
to the fierce monsoon wind
in the middle of nowhere,
there is dust in my eyes now.

i can't really see.

how can i know you
if you hide yourself
away from me
in the swirl of blowing dust?

i can't really see.

union means nothing
in between,
but to you
every woman for herself.
my mind observes the two strangers
that we've become.

i can't really see.

i fumble for the everlasting
as you push away
toward deeper water.

sunrise

like bookends
your arms maintain
our perfect alignment.

the night passes quickly
as the sun begins to lift
above the morning's horizon.

in the pinkness of our room
i watch your lips
move over my body.

half awake i recognize
your gentle caress.
i know that love exists.

the perfectly powered stars
disappear until later,
for now, we lay
together to watch the sun rise.

the guest

in a tranquil song
i listen to her grace
breathe this glorious light
into my house, i stay
and she blankets me
with raw passion.

the presentation of light

close to sunrise
i wake with you inside
my mind, my heart.
shades and shadows
don't exist.
full spectrum intoxication
with the gradual return of light.
you fill me with excitement,
a giddyness, a dance.
we are clowns of spirit
skipping along the path.
i lose myself, fully,
inside of this fire,
this relationship.
whatever it is,
incomprehensible,
whatever it will be.
we don't know.
it repeats.
we just feel it.
joy, passion, heat, light.
just a favorite song plays over and over.
i am overwhelmed, transported.
this brightness that will not be dimmed.
the entire world is lit
by this kind of love.

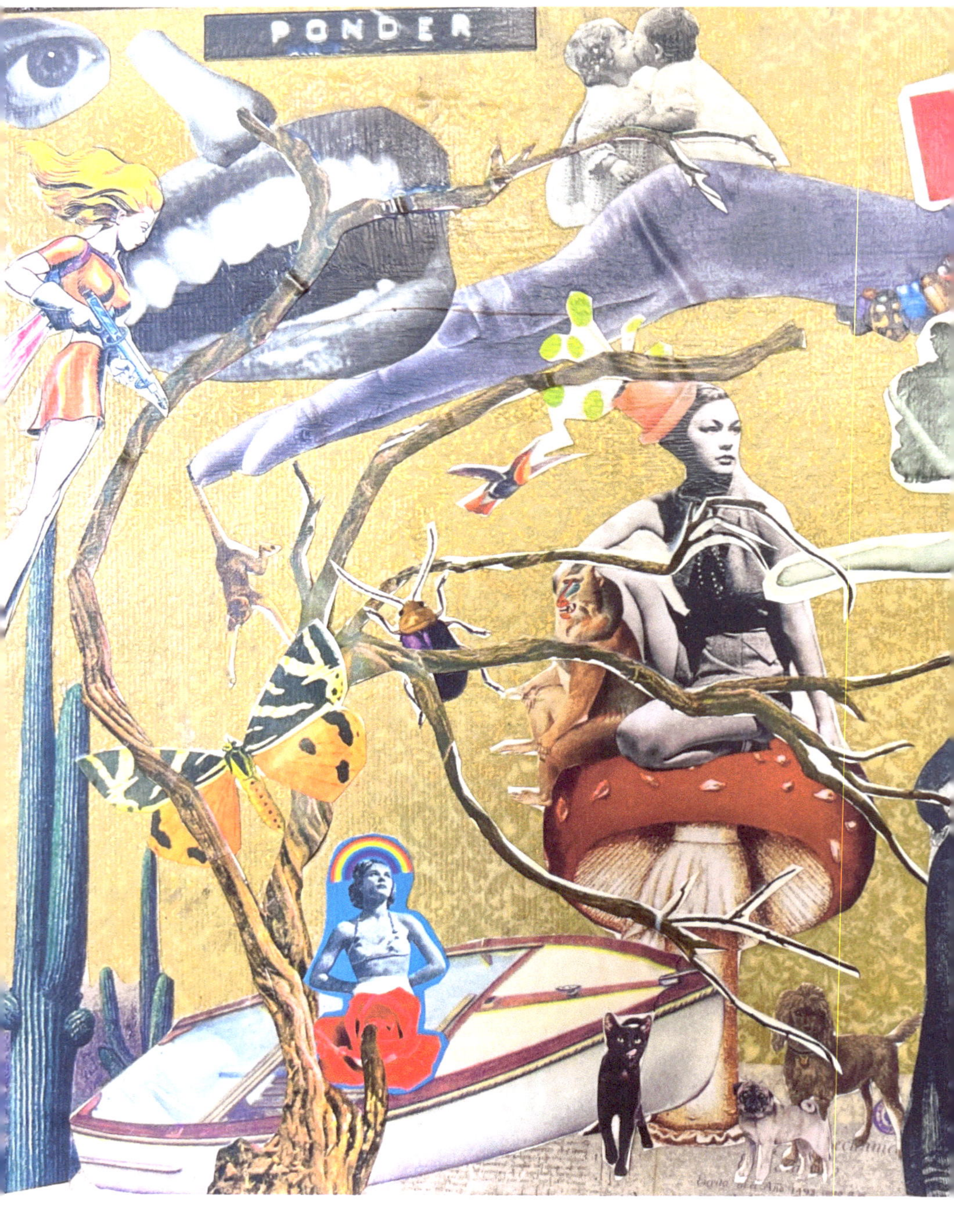

PONDER

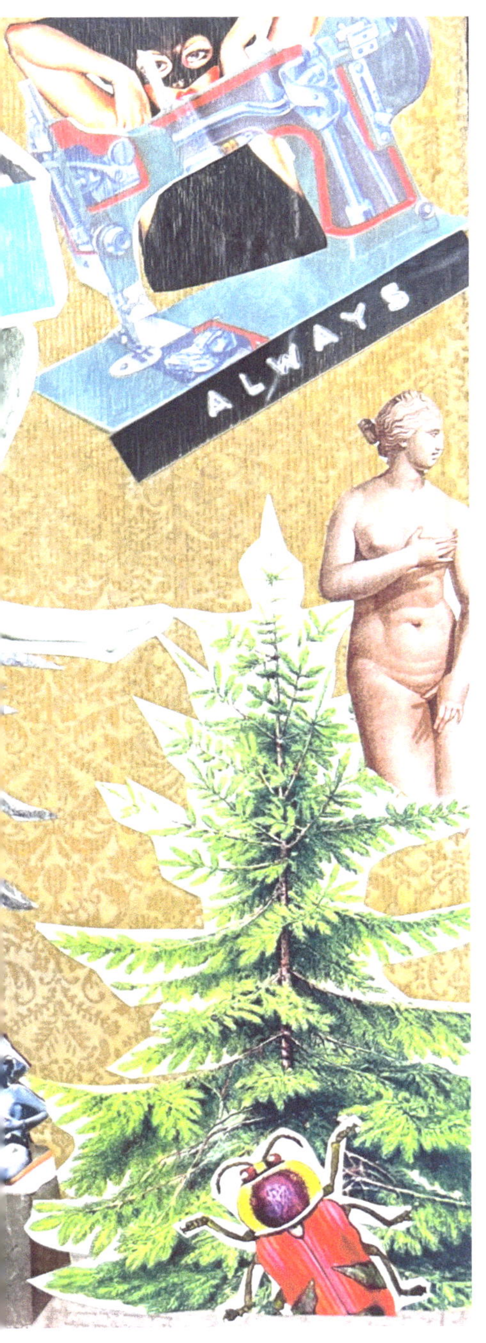

kaitlyn

in the year gone by
the force of mother nature
continues to call
composing her new shape.

does she look in the mirror
and see her
beautiful self?

as i stare at her i wonder
if she knows that
in a few short years
her phone will be
ringing off the hook?

her smile
so big -
a smile that grips my heart
and sings its new song.

her freedom and independence
remind me of my own youth -
and without knowing it
she tosses her hair
toward the wind.

she has learned respect and
appreciates kindness
kaitlyn loves, unconditionally
she comforts my ills
and brightens my darkest moments.

she gives incredible light
to becoming a mother.

the sweatshirt poem

to protect me
i wear this cloth
that you wore last
against your skin

it smells like you
and keeps me warm
tonight

i placed myself alone
where all i have is my brain
listening to my beating heart

a cloud bursts
between my legs

i wear this cloth

uncovered

it's because of you.

the struggle to find shelter
has ended.
i'm still standing though
and i've set down my guard.

from an unsettled mind
to the woman
now walking in my shoes
i can identify so clearly
who i am.

when you call my name
i bask in the sound of your voice,
it is when you hold me still,
that i am free.

in uncovering this truth
distinguishing my own pulse,
i have also found the safe place
to dwell within your heart.

thirst

abused, empty woman
waits for fulfillment

she sleeps wide awake
the whole night through
dancing around shadows
tossing and turning
around another lifetime

she imagines a sweeter way
but weakness has tied
her to darkness
though
appreciative of love
passionate about living

dehydrated, always
thirsty for more
too tired
to get up

she still lays in darkness
waiting for morning
and her everlasting truth

this morning's imagery

horizontal light
peeking from the sky -
sends the rising sun
into one eye.

a mouthful of kisses
coming your way
a heart full of joy
to help you start your day.

good morning, my love
in each day i've found
happiness
that together we're bound.

i tell you now
as i have before you,
i must have
forever and more.

the juice is poured
the cereal soggy -
i must be dreaming
everything's foggy.

> i lay awake now
> staring at the wall
> no wonder -
> no answer
> there's no one here at all.

this is the way

you walk across my thoughts
and swirl in my mind
as the leaves this fall

we decide
that there is no better place
for us -
than together

we kiss
as if our neighbors
don't drive by here

we make no apologies
for our happiness
or the life
that we want -

or the change of the seasons

winter walk

there is chaos
in these woods
on a day like today
you dally
with my heart

your mouth,
the jawline of the woods,
moves
so your lips touch mine

the cold of your skin
brushes against
my chin, delicate breasts
i borrow from time
this moment

i want to marry
for better ...

what's new

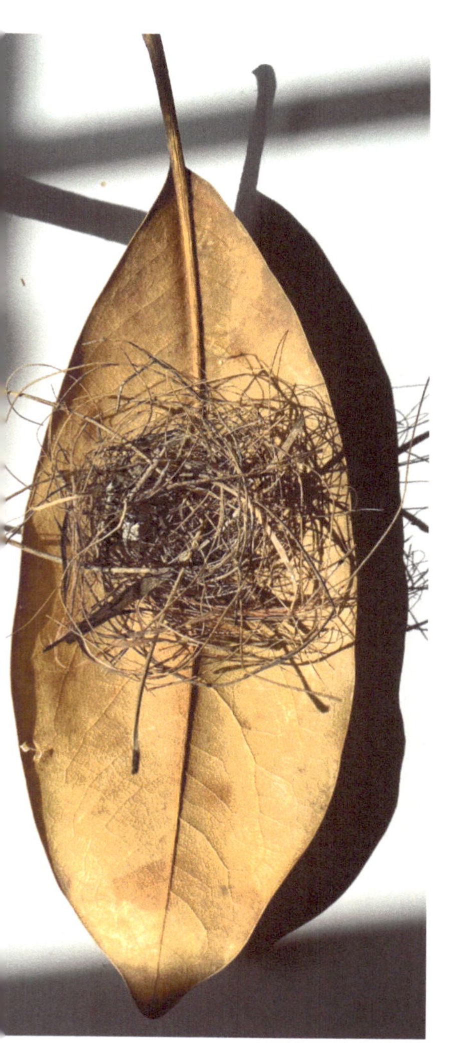

today it may rain
tomorrow i will be gone
on my way to meet with you again
i keep no secrets now
but i will tell you about my life
share with you
my dreams and current news
i've kept far from you
what's new
something perhaps
        i will never understand
people heard about us
usually together
someone like you
a special friend
it would take years to discover
i'm afraid someday
i'll be without you for real
when our lives end
and then
it will be too late
to say i'm sorry

why climb trees

silence
seems a lot
like climbing a tree

perching
branch by branch
to see it all   then

                       when you
                       reach the top
                       the view has vanished

                       silence
                       climbing high
                       just to land on ground

silk lips

my heart is exhilarated
listening to her body

i feel her reach
for me
her lips as silk
cling

her wet mouth
re-hydrates me
after being apart

moments flash
like a train ride

reminding me
of how much
i need to be
in her presence

behind the waterfall

skin to skin
like my favorite song
you lift me up
we dance and shiver.
my soul flame
since the very first night
high tide, low tide
through it,
all of it
side by side.
just the gulls
over my head
miles make no difference.
i felt your hands
in the night
and as i wake.
a dream
so wild, untamed
you set me free.
my body wide open, calm
wet.
these dreams
are my vacation.
a smile crosses my lips
into the day
i take

anticipated warmth

from the first kiss
a special place for your nose
on my face.
from the first glance
a fire stoked inside me,
igniting a spark.

your eyes touch me
where no one has ever been -
no one else may ever go.
as a wildfire
awake and alive,
my heart
after the first kiss,
lives outside its wildest dream.

the contour of your cheek
pressing into mine
torching warmth meets
lips wet from the first kiss.

you lift your hand to touch me
eyes slightly shut
this first kiss
consumes my heart -

nothing between you and me
but the first kiss.

cafe portrait

i recall
brilliant breasts
in peach linen

her subtle curves
just out of reach

light embraces
bare belly
and moves downward
out of my sight

my uninterrupted stare
caught her eye

i wonder
who may have seen
her touch me

without touching me at all

the vortex

in the moment
where the heart is
things are good.

indeed, i go one day at a time.
what's important
reveals itself
at every second.

every step takes me
closer to the top
of the mountain.

perched in the grand entryway
of the chapel of the holy cross
i stare across the peaks
to see mother and child
the madonna
perfectly etched
into royal blue sky.

i pray
the moment my life ends
i end up here,
my forever home.
it is where my heart is,
my beginning and
my end.

                what's important
                in my silent pause,
                always reveals itself
                on top of this mountain.

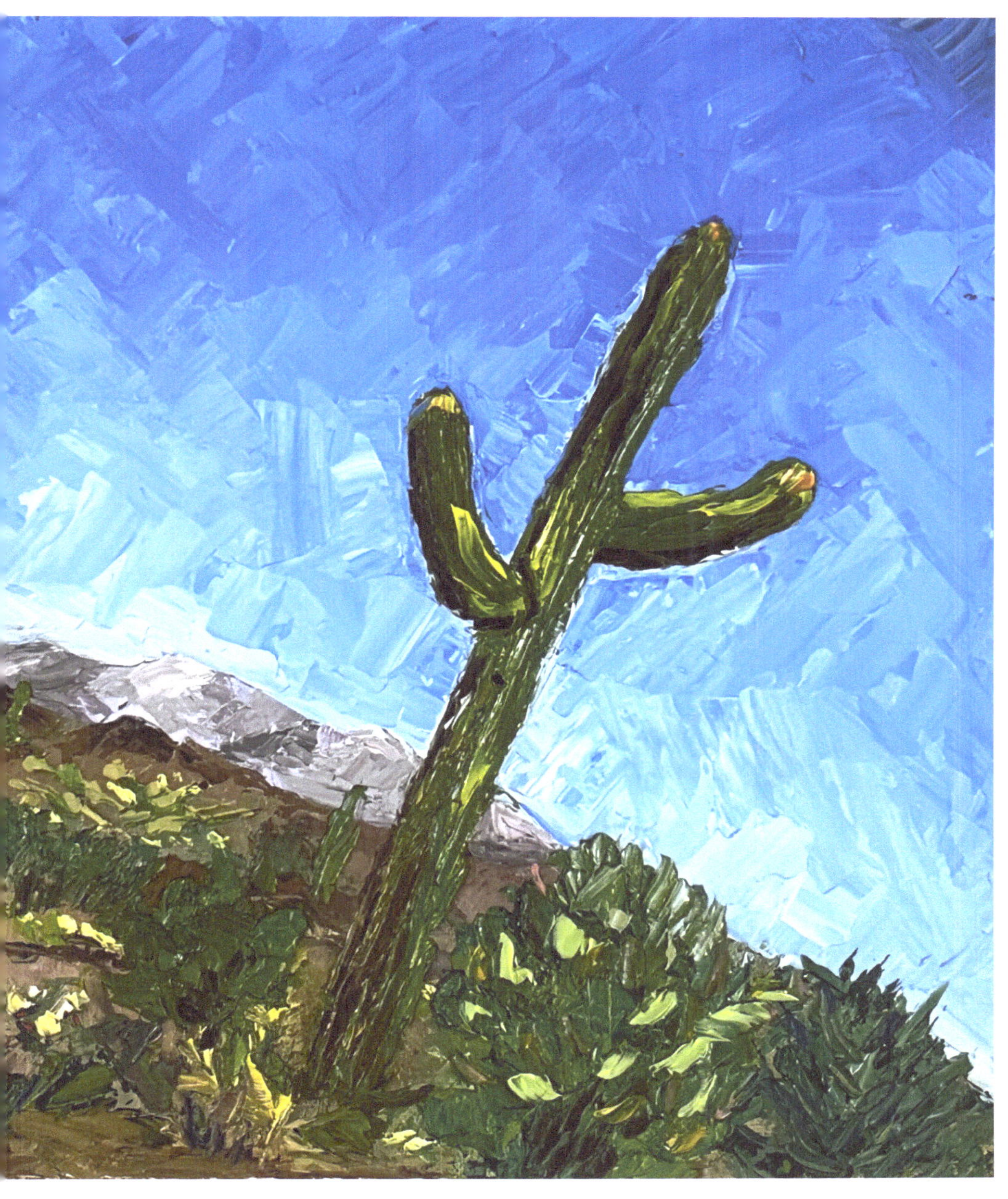

i will return to this place
right here
in a million little pieces
one final pilgrimage
to be one with
this universal magnificence.

cultivating sexuality

we don't
talk about
it

though i can plant mine
anywhere
i dig
and die -
here

bypassing old roots
and rocks
along the way

i've grown to adrnire
the shadow
of myself

i labor in love
nourishing
tiny sprouts
of sexuality

divine tears

love
the rhythm
of our eyes
opening and closing,
our bodies waltzing.
my eyes explode
the joyous tears
my heart overflows.

in a moment

i wonder what it would feel like
to kiss you.

to daydream of our bodies
together, early on sunday morning.

what if we made love a hundred times
and never felt tired
nor thirsty
or into what's on tv?

just us
soaking in the moment

perhaps words
would not even be necessary.

erotic sky

i wondered which cloud
on the other side of town
you might be under.
i'm here- you there;
how far my dreams have traveled
across the erotic sky.

heavy on my mind,
would you grace me
with that magic?
when will i feel the warmth
of your breath?

i wonder how our thoughts
get connected
in the middle of my day?
quietly, i consider the body's
urge to cling.

erotic sky,
i'm not afraid
of the thunder
any longer.

i'm wet
like the flowers
just after the rain.

sweet and lovely
i will kiss her
as the clouds decide
to clear.

finding shelter

the struggle to find shelter
has ended,
from my mind
to the woman that
now fills my shoes.

i can see now
who I am suppose to be
because of you.

when you call my name
i go crazy
after you've gone
i go crazy
finding the truth in my shoes
it's becomes easier
to live with myself,
to balance the life line
i should have uncovered
so long ago.

i go crazy
for not finding shelter
in your heart
before now.
my favorite gift
finding the sunshine
on your smile.

first pantoum

i like the way she opens up
just like a flower
in the middle of the night
three am
just like a flower
her lips - warm against my neck
three am
her body grips my hand
lips warm against my neck
four am
we connect
her body grips my hand
four am
breathing intuitively
we connect
infinity, at last
breathing intuitively
in the middle of the night
infinity, at last
i like the way she opens up

full moon frenzie

i borrow some time
from a poem
to remember what
 it feels like.
ahh, to feel
the rise and fall
of a lover's chest
out of breath after
after hours of making love

i imagine
panels of cloudy
shattered windows,
no one loves anymore.
some throw stones
without even looking

i hope you got
what you came for
friendship, new love
the goodnight kiss.

somewhere
beneath the distant sky
my tears fade away
into the moonlight

i borrow, i imagine
i wonder, i hope ...

full moon brings a
sleepless night
so i read erotica

i wonder what
you look like
with the sun in your face?

little boy pleasures

on the side yard
we chose our teams
all those boys
took me
last

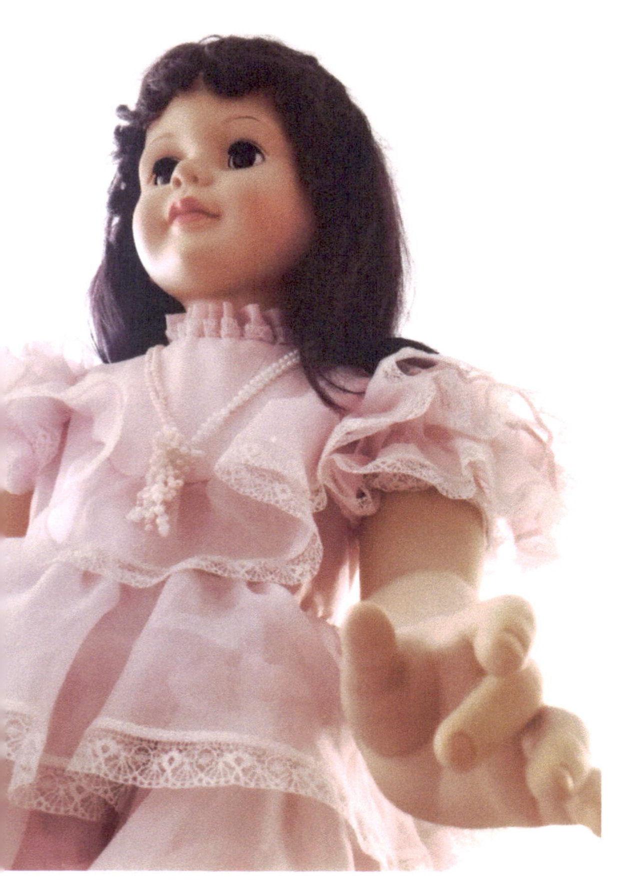

little boy pleasures
of crossing the creek
in one wide jump
playing bat-ball and
racing bikes

we feed worms to fishhooks
and have a
construction company

we tortured so many dolls
cut their hair
and twisted their heads

they lay
buried in the yard
with their passion
to be played with

little girls

they giggle
                    "i don't mind about you
                    if you don't mind about me."

they make squirmy faces
touching cheeks, noses and tongues

tonight their laughter
turns my eyes
to tears
because
i am not that little girl

that's what's funny -
they can giggle
for years
before anyone catches on

without many tears
slipping by

never hanging up

i sent
postcards in the summer
in those days
you collected them
i remember
our sticky hands
picking crab apples
and twisting the stems

our kisses
amateur of course
hiding in the hallway
where no one could see
       somehow i knew
       that i'd end up
       the same
       with you loving me
all those days
i wondered
how people change
how would we have known
       i'm glad to see you now
       because we are the same
       and every time you call
       i still can't hang up the phone

spread to the edge

the words in my head
are similar to those i wrote
twenty-some years ago,
mostly about finding my self.
from my first husband
i learned about shredding carrots -
lots and lots of carrots.
and from the second
how to make the perfect
peanut butter and jelly sandwich -
with the peanut butter spread
all the way to the edge.
many of these outbursts
still buzz around in my head.
i seek the perfect love
just as i had thirty five years ago -

the strong street

remembering the nights
       we'd lay upon the warm street
       after the sun had gone,
       back to back

i gasp to grab my breath
       the beautiful moment
       had stolen

tonight as any other
       we'd wonder
       where all the years had gone
       that we'd spent in the street

when all voices ceased
       to an unbearable silence
       we'd announce
       to our dear ftiends
       it's time to go inside

the strong street holds our secrets
       some painted boundaries
       that old fallen willow

       and the
       broken
       lines
              i've always wanted
              to write.

t.g.i.f.

had an idea of beginning somewhere
            to versify my thoughts

what words shall i blend
            with so many possible choices

there's something inside me

fierce and pulverizing
            that cannot be resolved
i woke in the middle of last night
            with a complete stanza
            didn't want to wake you with light
i am on the edge it seems,
            of what?
this is not a billet-doux but
            merely an expression
don't be distressed or concerned
            at each moment
            someone's life becomes absent.

that tree ate my donut

that tree in the backyard is mine
but ted says it's his 'cause it's right on the line

we sit and talk
and do things kids do
each day
something new

we burn worms with a magniffing glass
in the sun
or make the neighborhood kid
eat mud and berries
'cause we think he's dumb

we made a jump with some bricks
and with our bikes
did some tricks

yesterday we had some donuts
and when we got here today
they were out of sight
that tree must have eaten them
late last night

the sacred space of my bedroom

one tear
drifts beyond my ear
and joins the others
on my pillow

just one life
one breath
and one body
in our sacred space

heat and energy
rush over me
emptying my lungs
of its breath

i feel as good as gold
and smile wide

cello and piano
fill the silence
making me want more

the cat sits quiet
not knowing
whether to go or stay

he stays
listening to the music

the unsaid

you, me
the blink of an eye,
sudden passion,
infinite love -

so many nights
i dream
of laying close to you -
no wonder
of where you end
or where I begin.

strangers
bound together in spirit,
love,
and all the stuff
souls are made of.

things are different now

mom called to chat.
things are different now.
things are different now.
without any kids in the house, she said.
your father walks through the kitchen
in his underwear.
i imagine he is probably pushing against her
at the sink as we speak.
he makes her late for work now.
flowers appeared for no particular reason
and even does the dishes now and then.
things are just different now, she said.

we agree that cracke jack prizes aren't worth a damn,
one of our third cousins started to kiss us right on the lips,
and butterfingers just don't taste the same -
things are different now.

your addiction

why do you think
i live in a fantasy world?

is it because i write love letters
or because i believe the rain is coming
when the cows are laying down?
i don't think it's so strange
to want to decipher what license plates say.

maybe you think i am crazy
because i talk to trees
or because i like to lick the snow
or maybe it's because i like soaring
the desert skies in search
of new mountains to climb.

or, is it that i live
in a fantasy world
because i'd like
every day to be
loving you?

just because

i'd rather eat chocolate ice cream today
than pay my bills.

rather make wishes to the full moon
than some far away star beyond the hill.

while i'd like to be emily dickinson
and be comfortable in a dress,

i prefer the echo of a golden bell
to that feeling that lingers in my chest.

much more i'd enjoy the scent of lavender
than being cheated a day of precious time.

rather than a weak and lonely branch
i wish to resemble the strongest, lush vine.

i choose to sit in the middle of the creek
to listen as the water arrives,

at times i'd rather be dead
than only half alive.

girlish volume

my childhood sits
clealry on my mind
far enough away
but close enough to remind me
some raisins and orange juice
a song of football plays
right around the bend from here
i hear it every day

dull

dull the morning sky
wating for its sun to rise
i've nothing to fear

far off land

i'm building a boat
animals board first
the mice, lions
and doves

peace and security
may save me
from this flood

i pull the covers
overhead
and shout
all aboard

time
is for me
to discover

bindings

i know other people
must have this condition

the one of collecting books

many books line my four walls
they have become part of me
perhaps a protective layering
of information

all of my knowledge
is lined up in between the pages
waiting for my attention
once more

i delve into the story
behind each story
books are precious
and passionate
personal and essential

these books are my foundation
my inner grounding

i consider the piles of papers
other people gather
or the laundry that mounds
in the corner

maybe they have one too many
junk drawers in the kitchen

continuance

tonight
i notice
a vein
dancing
on my
thigh

disappointment
amplified
by fear

promised beauty
now broken

i wish
too much
to change
myself

and not
grow
older

i do this
late in the evening a
almost every night -

i sink into bed

     hoping that my mind will just

   stop

peaceful space

with my feet perched
flat against a rock
i sit in the middle of the creek.
i cross my hands
and beg the earth
for energy.

i close my eyes for a moment
to listen for the message
the flowing water might bring.

i hear the water run into the rock
next to where i am seated -
its path changes, for some reason,
and forces the water
toward another place.

i am flexible,
understanding that
there is a path
for me
free of attachments -
and pain.

—— i center my attention
not on my obstacles
but on my breath,
life force,

i carefully watch the water
being carried to another place -
a more calm and peaceful place
down the creek,
realizing that there must be
a more peaceful space
waiting for me too.

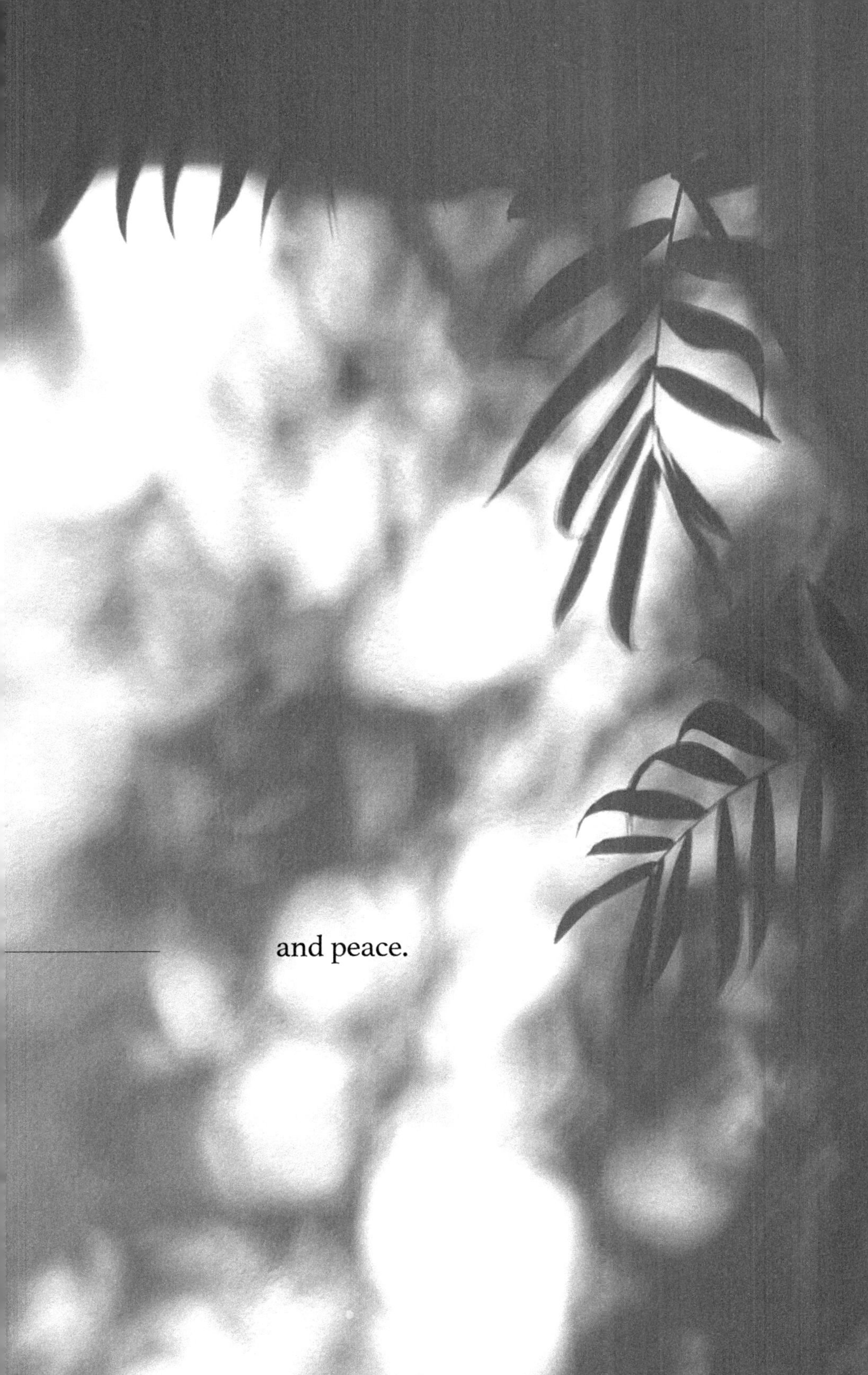
and peace.

it's christmas again

grandmother
i can hear your laughter
gently guiding our day.

it's like you stand to the side of me
passing gifts
and time.

you whisper the tale
but young children can't hear you.
they spin and make circles
around and around
the christmas tree -

wishing the old fashioned christmas,
the ones in which you were present,
had never gone away.
they don't like it now
because you've gone.

tear filled eyes
and the space in our hearts
is where you stay.

life teaching

everyone points a finger
and laughs
as i skip along the shore

i stare back
as the waves crash
and children scream

i find nothing good enough,
clean enough
or even sweet enough

i walk along the beach
searching and praying
to find my way

i forget
so i pretend

i want
and want -
so i give in

i sit in the water
with the sand

and look for myself
inside a shell

emotional blessing

our consciousness determines
our openness to receive.
emotions on repeat
like cells reproducing.

feelings that are rejected
and torn down by someone else.
they are on repeat
like loud, unpleasant music.
my heart bleeds
and screams out for love
affection, and understanding.

i become violent toward myself.
so easily misaligned
by someone else's energy.
must release
anger, rejection and self-hatred.

i know
in my heart
that i deserve good,
all the good.
there is more wholeness
than time.

———————————————

my desires run deep
and influence my days.
i learn to walk away
better
stronger
and fully awake.

thoughts affect the body.
everything is connected
and influenced
by what we are created to do.

abundance

though a human creation
i am of divine spirit.

nature provides freedom
and the universe is mine.

i live in love and creative thought.

each moment i celebrate
my abundant heart,
rich consciousness,
and my dedication is simple.

quiet is the mind
whose heart is pure -

my awareness, complete.
truth is visible
to those who can see.

each day
i come clean.

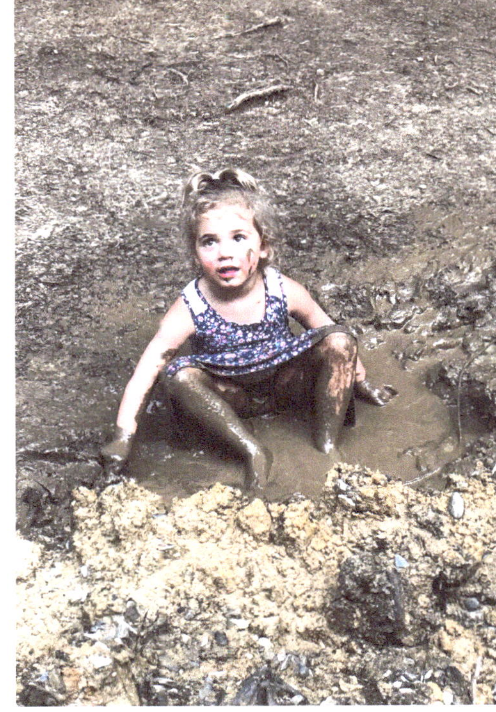

winter morning

still mind
soft breath
quiet heart -
promise rest.

an open mind
changing shape
form and flexibility -
pure tranquility

mystic female
both colorful and clear
unmoving eyes -
pure soul i peer

no longer bound
by want or desire
confusion lost -
in a magical fire.

soft breath
uncharted way
this meditation
unfolds another day.

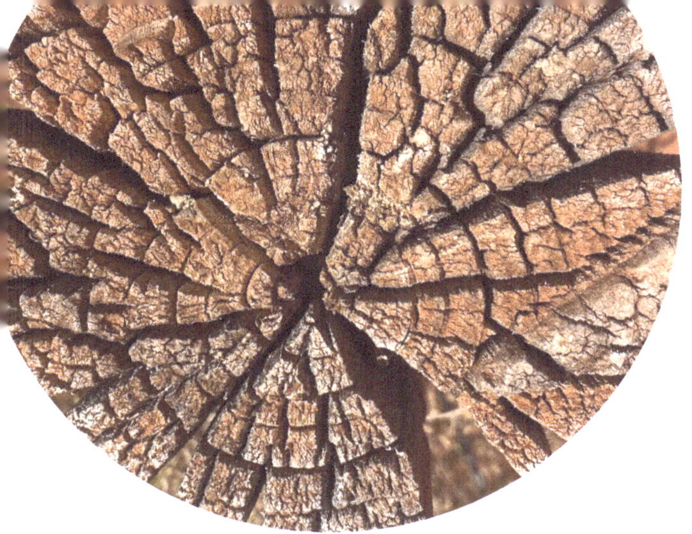

native spirit

shades of fire
settle across the sky
filtered sun
highlights red rock

i study
the broken lines
she left behind

engraved by hand
into the mountainside

tradition she knew
i'd someday find

though i am alone
native spirit moves me

i dance and rejoice
in her inspirational echoes

travel

empty mind
and energy flow
onto a page full of words,
heart and mind connection
swallowed up

traveling,
blooming like a flower
i rest my head on your shoulder
in the full sun
until darkness disappears

passion
somehow makes its way
into my broken heart
without me even knowing it

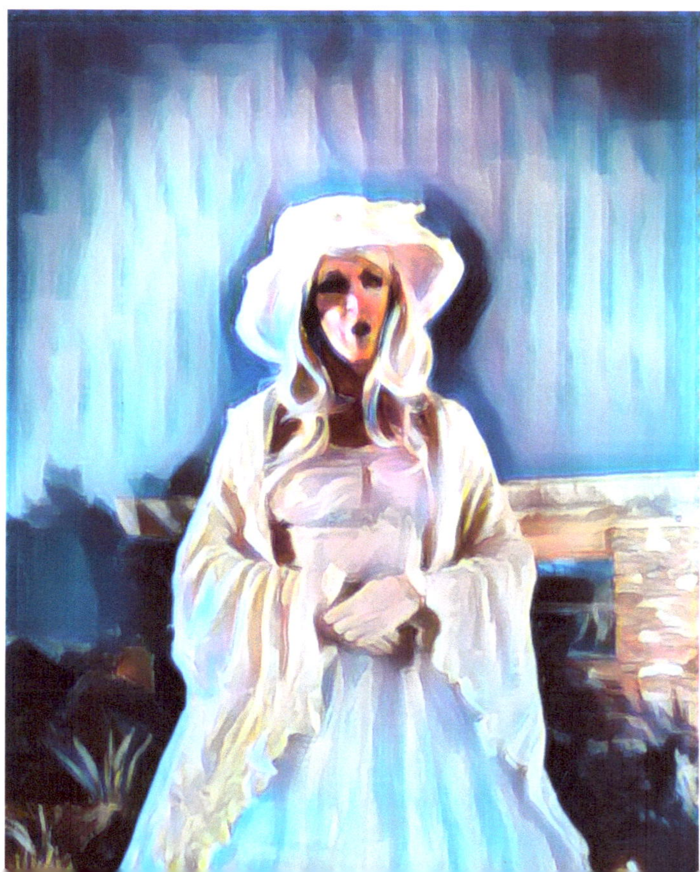

chameleon

look! the man i have seen a thousand times
in the movies and on tv
is walking along the street.

he carts a loaded pack
and a cigarette dangles
from his rigid jaw.
hair pulled tight
from his worn and weathered skin
still, he uses the morning's sunrise
to soothe his battle scars.

he appears to be content,
confident and invincible
while inside he scoots and scampers,
craving more.

from where i am
i watch him scurry.
i wonder his story
and feel him suffer.

the desert is commonplace
for chameleons
who are pulled out west
by some divine, healing force.

i wonder how many miles he will travel
before he realizes that walking away
will not take him where he wants to go?

spiritual balance

some days it is easy
to let time slip by
some men never embrace
or ever find tears to cry.

unkept promises and
friends
we forget to meet are the
unkept stars
that explode in our sleep.

so many longings
inside of our heads
still we crash our cars

and sit
on the edge of our beds.

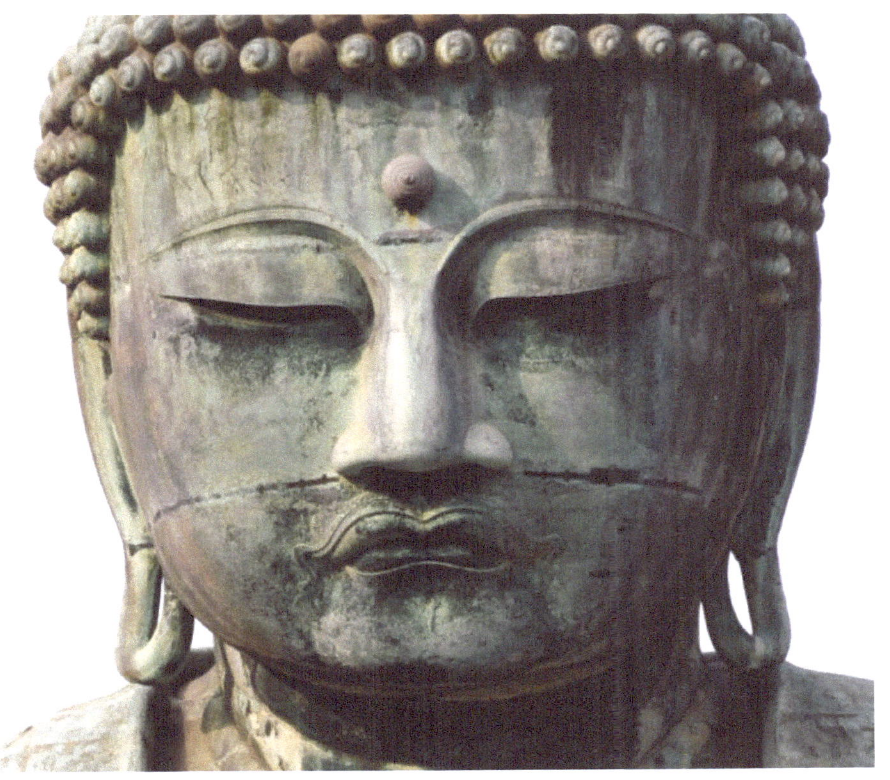

153

garden helper

today i saw a robin.
she pointed out to me
new leaves on the maple tree
and some on the oak.
the little flowers blooming underneath
crocus and daffodils
i bend down to poke.
spring is the time to get out my rake
to clean up the garden again.
i waited all winter
for the season to come.
we must take away old leaves,
fallen sticks
and left over winter remains.
once the soil is showing
i dig to plant some seeds.
flowers here,
vegetables there,
whatever poppop needs.
being a helper in the garden
is a very important job.
our garden needs
sunlight, rain and
tender loving care.
in my free time
i bend over
to talk to the new plants.
i wish them well
and pray that
they grow strong.

holding peace

a poem is nothing less
than spirit
speaking through me

an overflow
of emotion
which is calmly recalled

together
we collect tranquility
narrate history
and passionate events

we don't succeed
until we've touched
someone's heart

poetry puts human life
into words

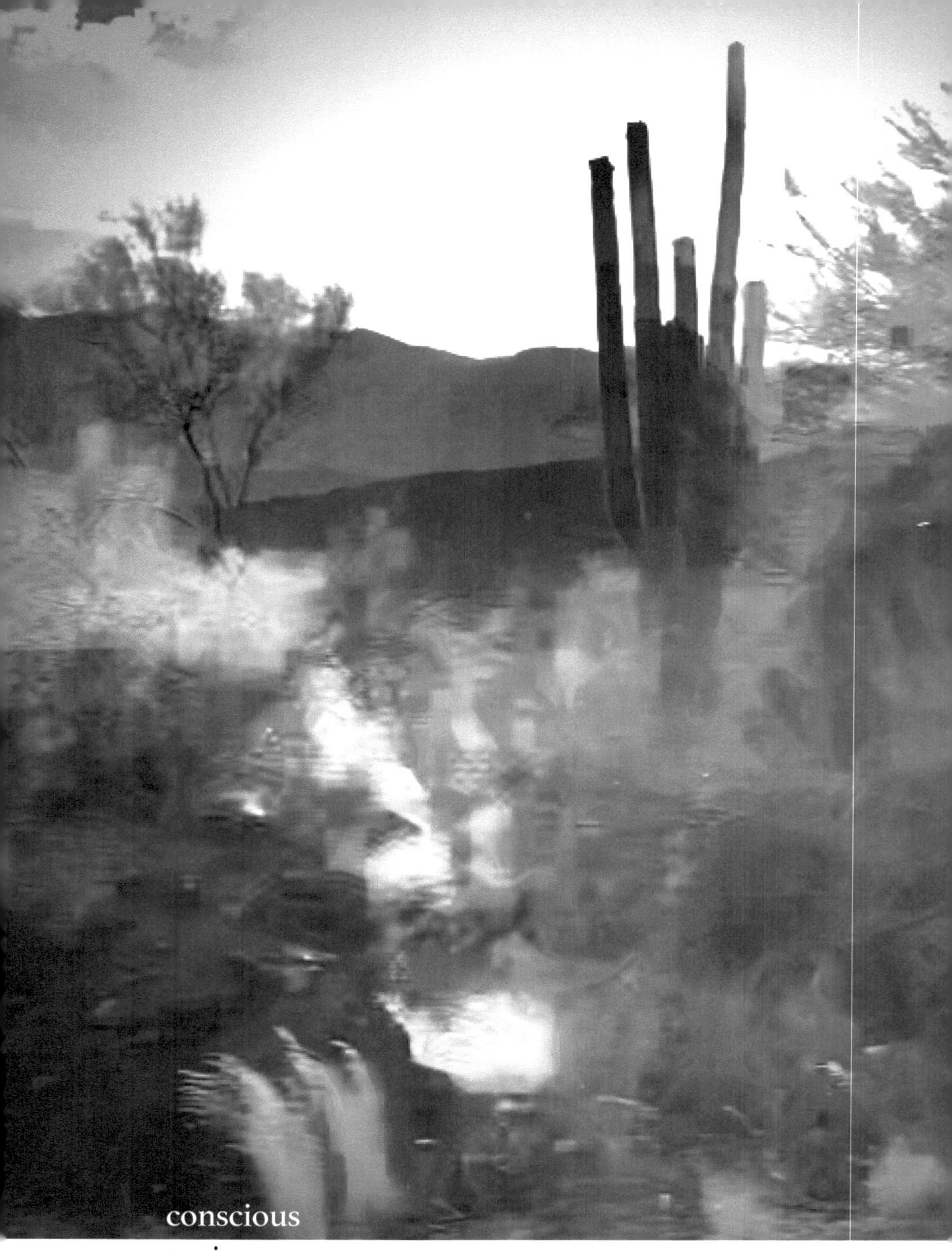
conscious
curious

sonoran heart

going to the desert.

time doesn't matter to me
cause i am two thousand miles
from nowhere,

conscious and curious,
there's no place
i'd rather be.

in the desert
i am happy to stand
on my own.

this sonoran sun
can rise up
and come down on me,
again and again

until i disappear.

Karen Izzi, PhD

Since she was six years old, Izzi has been writing, journaling, making art, sewing, and poking at dead things with a stick. At a very young age, she stood on a chair and learned to cook with her Grandmother. Izzi is a metaphysician, mixed media artist, caregiver, educator, potter, former stylist, and poet. She believes in the power of love. She is an advocate for nature, the equality of all people and animals. Izzi has been seen hugging trees and getting up close and personal with bugs, birds, plants, and flowers.

Izzi founded Conscious Creations Art Studio in 2012, on a mission to support and promote other artists and writers within the community. Izzi is a Certified Alzheimers Caregiver. She is a member of several botanical gardens, SAQA, NCECA, Arizona Art Alliance, the American Art Therapy Association and realizes that the power of art therapy and writing changes everything. She has been published in a variety of national/international publications. As a student of meditation and a teacher of Zentangle®, a method of pen-to-paper meditation. Izzi loves to meet and connect with like-minded people.

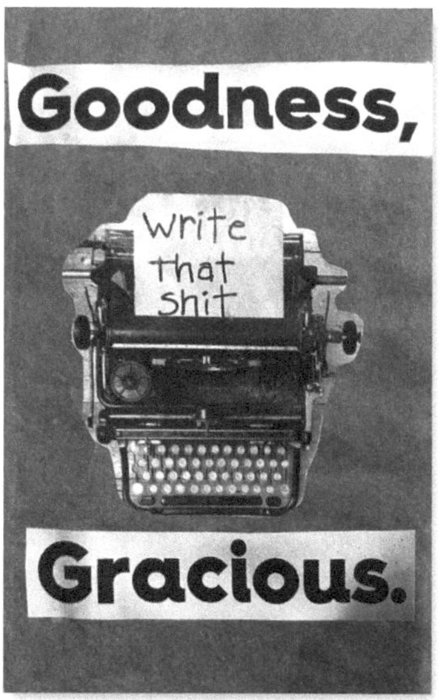

She encourages everyone to live to their fullest potential, every single day.

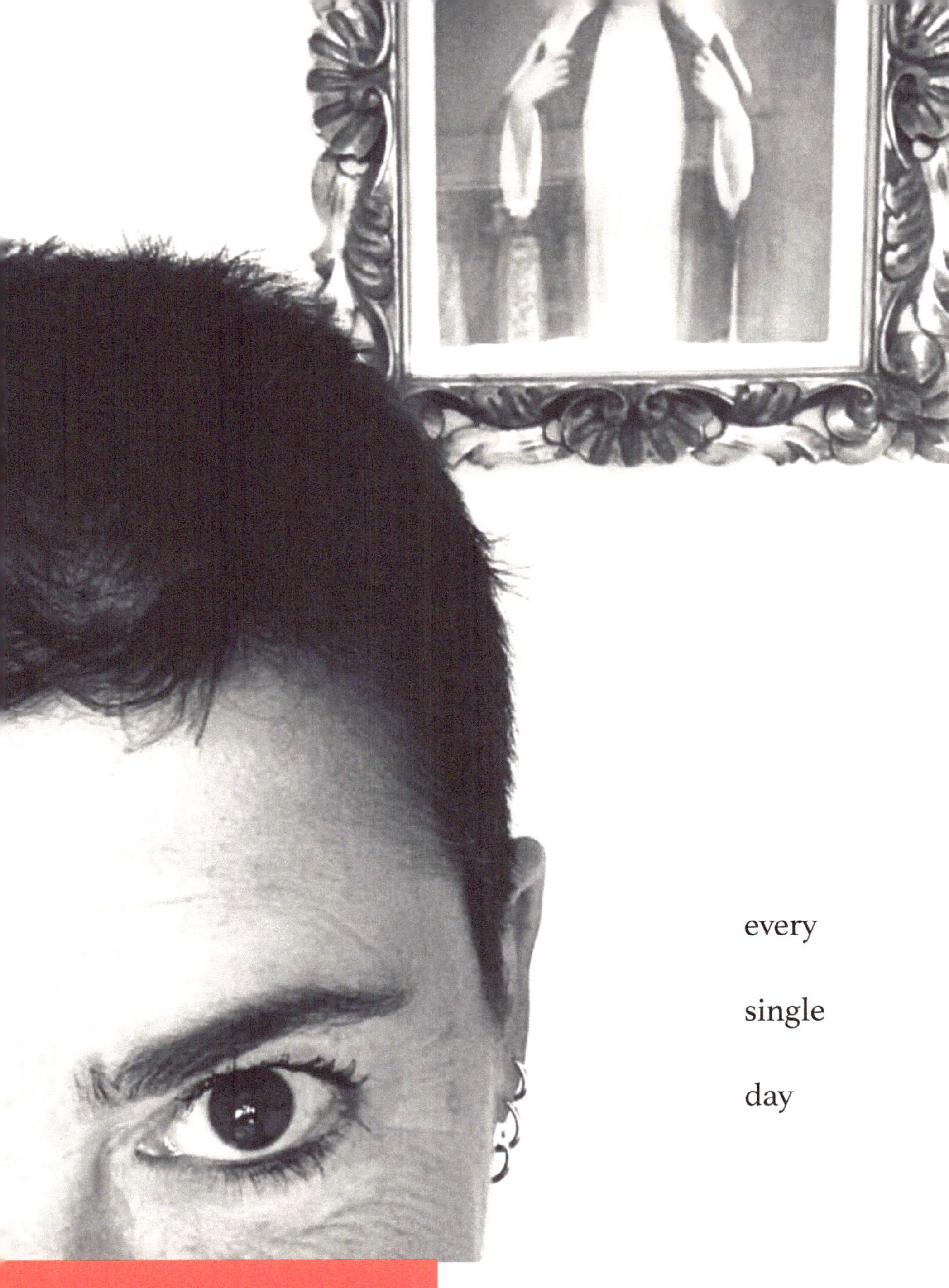

every

single

day

ARTISTIC HOSLISTIC

the final page

on the edge of what feels right
and wrong
i sit with this journal
as my emotions hold it hostage.

what feels like a lifetime of desire -
a thirst somehow quenched
i hunger, no more.
today i catch myself
taking extra time
feeling as if i am pretty.

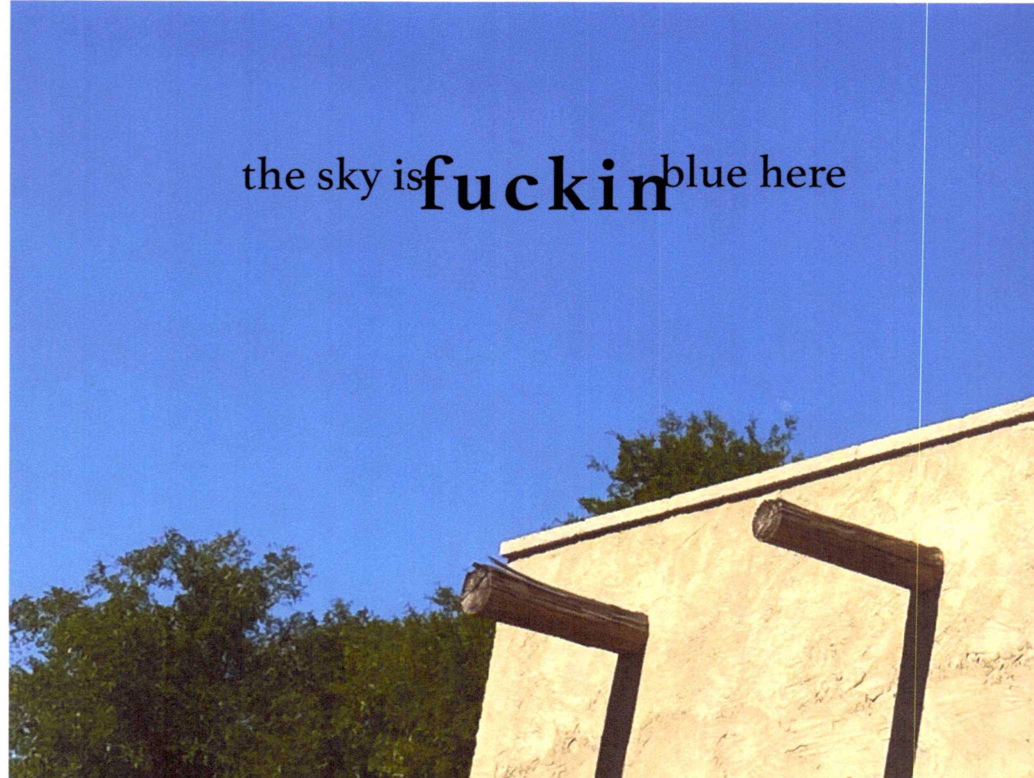

i look for you in traffic
like i will see you pull up
right next to me
and smile -
that great smile.

just before i turn the page
i realize
this last page
could be the best one yet.

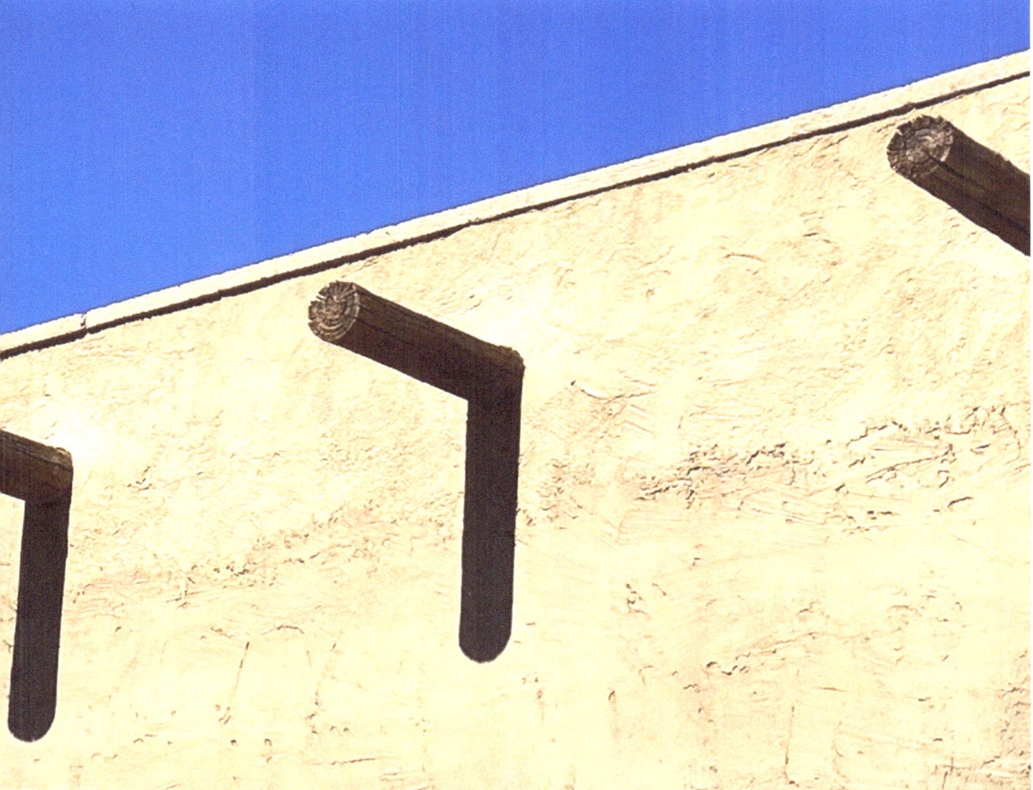

9 780578 690186